Dancing with Destiny

Turning Points on the Journey of Life

Sharon Wegscheider-Cruse

Health Communications, Inc.
Deerfield Beach, Florida

www.hci-online.com

Pages 9-11 from *Peace, Love and Healing* by Bernie S. Siegel, M.D.
Copyright ©1989 by Bernard S. Siegel, M.D.
Reprinted by permission of HarperCollins Publishers, Inc.

Library of Congress Cataloging-in-Publication Data

Wegscheider-Cruse, Sharon, date.
  Dancing with destiny: turning points on the journey of life /
Sharon Wegscheider-Cruse.
     p.   cm.
  Includes bibliographical references.
  ISBN 1-55874-457-6 (trade paper)
  1. Spiritual life. 2. Experience (Religion) 3. Self-realization
—Religious aspects. I. Title.
BL624.W3844   1997
291.4—dc21   96-52296
                                                     CIP

©1997 Sharon Wegscheider-Cruse
ISBN 1-55874-457-6

All rights reserved. Printed in the United States of America. No part of this publication may be reproduced, stored in a retrieval system or transmitted in any form or by any means, electronic, mechanical, photocopying, recording or otherwise without the written permission of the publisher.

Publisher: Health Communications, Inc.
             3201 S.W. 15th Street
             Deerfield Beach, FL 33442-8190

Cover illustration by Larissa Hise
Cover design by Lawna Patterson Oldfield
Cover background photo © Jim Zuckerman

*I dedicate this book to
my fellow travelers who have used
"turning points" in their lives to more clearly
recognize their personal destinies.
Those of you who have contributed
to this book and many others who have
shared their stories with me have
helped shape my understanding of the
"Dance with Destiny."*

Contents

Acknowledgments ix
Introduction: Welcome to the Dance xi

Part One: Learning to Dance

Dancing Lessons: The Basics 3
Divine Protection 5
   Topped-Off Travel 6
   The Right Side of Town 7
   Red Rose of Texas 8
Spiritual Truths 11
One Step at a Time 13
   I Asked 14
   Out of the Mouths of Babes 16
   A Loving Spoonful 16
Miracles 19
   The Fire 22
   The Gift of Tears 23
Lost and Found 27
   She Offered Me Hope 29
   Love Power 29

Prayer and Meditation 31
   The Prayer Table 32
   The Voice of a Guardian Angel 33
   The God Box 34
The One and Only 35
   Gratitude 36
   Single Mom's Reward 36
   The Healing Touch 37
Discernment 39
   You Get Back What You Give Away 41
   Butterflies Lift Spirits 41
   The Colonel 42
Born to Dance 43

Part Two: Transformations of the Heart

Becoming One with Our Destiny 47
   One Healer, One Story 48
   That's Life 55
   Death and Rebirth of a Soul 59
   The Physiology of Love, Joy and Optimism 63
   A Second Chance 67
   I Wanted a Relationship 71

**Part Three: Transformation: Becoming More
of Who We Are**

The Body, Mind and Spirit 77
   The Sign 80
   Al-Anon's Message 81
The Patterns of Transformation 83
   Bureaucracy 84
   A Safe Place 85

Contents vii

Transforming People..................................87
Relationships and Transformation.................89
Comfort in Verse...............................92
An Angel in Adversity 92
Seeking Balance High and Low.....................95
The Dance.....................................98
Meditation...99
Dreaming....................................100
The Meaning of Life..............................101
Faith Goes with the Flow.........................105
Swan Lake...................................108
A Good Time to Grow 111
A Short Visit from a Small Angel............112
Turning Points...................................115
Happy Birthday!.............................117
Computer Angel.............................118

Part Four: Transformations of the Soul

The Gift of Pain 123
Out of Pain, Joy............................127
Pass It On..................................131
Living on the Edge of Acceptance............134
We Are Never Alone..........................139
Moving into the Moment 141
Life Is a Do-It-Yourself Project 144
The Birth of a Butterfly 148

**Part Five: Messengers, Mentors and Teachers:
Modern-Day Prophets in the Everyday World**

When the Student Is Ready, the Teacher
  Will Appear...................................155

Tough Love..................156
You Never Know..................158
Religion and Spirituality..................159
A Letter to Loved Ones..................160
Unique Destinies, Unique Guides..................163
An Act of Kindness..................165
Angels Hang Stars of Hope..................166
My Own Angels..................169
Mentors and Teachers..................171
Second Chances..................172
Becoming a Messenger..................175
The Mystery of Angels..................177
A Musical Angel..................179

Part Six: Transformations of the Spirit

Honesty Isn't the Best Policy—It's the Only One...183
It's Not Your Fault..................186
Claiming My Power..................191
Becoming Whole Again..................195
The Beaver's Wand..................200
Motherhood: A Never-Ending Turning Point..................202
I Am Responsible for How I Feel..................206
Stop Wiggling..................209
Just Keep Walking..................215
Bottom of the Pit/Top of the Mountain..................218

Closure..................223
Bibliography..................225

Acknowledgments

A special thank you to:

The team at HCI. I especially appreciate Gary Seidler's support and belief in my work. Hats off to L. A. Justice for helping my words take form, and Christine Belleris, Matthew Diener and Mark Colucci for pulling the project together. A special thank you to my typist, Ellie Gore, and to Patrick Cotter, for his early editing.

The many people all over the United States who became my support team by sending me cards, letters, prayers, e-mail and flowers. Thank you, special angels. You know who you are.

Those people who share my daily life—my partner Joe, my children and their partners, and my six special grandchildren. You bless my life and are my greatest joy.

To my Higher Power whose protection I feel and whose direction in my life brings serenity and peace.

Introduction: Welcome to the Dance

Every natural fact is a symbol of some spiritual fact.

—Ralph Waldo Emerson

Signs of a spiritual revolution are everywhere as people in all walks of life, from every economic bracket, search for ways to transform their lives. They want to add meaning, contentment and inner peace to their humdrum lives.

The fixation on material goods, physical beauty, failed relationships and broken families, as well as the constant striving for financial success, has not nourished the souls of those searching for peace of mind, body and spirit.

A few cosmic travelers have found the depth of serenity

that comes from spiritual awareness. But for other searchers of truth, there is an awakening—a "turning point"—that begins the journey to transformation.

Sometimes the trigger is a sense of awe—the majesty of a snow-capped mountain, a crystal clear lake or stream, the scent of cinnamon, the sound of pine crackling in the fireplace at holiday time or the fresh, delicate fragrance of an infant, freshly bathed. These experiences can affect us profoundly and plant the seeds that make us want to unravel the mystery of life.

The unfolding comes in stages.

As our children grow—going from infancy to the first day of school, through the rites of passage, communion or bar mitzvah, to a first date, graduation, wedding or the birth of a child—we are touched by a powerful sense of life's steady yet irrepressible flow. We begin to see where we fit into the grand scheme of things.

Conversely, when we lose a parent or someone dearly loved, and we are forced to become the head of a family or network, the awareness becomes more acute. We are merely drops in a stream, circles in the trunk of a tree—part of something much more vast than we can ever be individually.

Nature has provided us with numerous ways to experience this feeling of grandeur. In the timeless cycle of spring blossoms and falling leaves, in the salt air and crashing surf of the seashore, we can embrace the certainty that life will go on, with or without us. While we are here, we can be part of nature, sense its strength and beauty, and feel reassured by its change-less, yet ever-changing ways. Nature is always willing

Introduction: Welcome to the Dance   xiii

to share serenity, yet it is always more powerful than our frail character.

As Eleanor Roosevelt once said: "Perhaps nature is our best assurance of immortality."

Awakening

In moments of clarity we can sometimes experience a jolt that causes us to wake up. Too often we don't understand the meaning of the sensation, we simply know we've been touched. When that happens, we question our purpose, our path and our understanding of life itself. We ask questions and begin to peek behind the cloak of mystery that surrounds our lives.

We know we are in the midst of a spiritual awakening when we ask more questions and have fewer pat answers; when we feel a hunger for understanding and our old frameworks and metaphors are not enough. When our old methods of trying to control life feel empty, it's time to search for more.

As we follow our hearts and savor the mysteries unfolding around us, life becomes exciting beyond our imagination. Material goods and concerns over money loosen their grip on our psyche and, instead, heartfelt experiences and connections bring new sparkle, fulfillment and inner peace to our souls.

As the awakening grows stronger, we begin to see signs that our path or journey has been laid out for us. We begin to reframe our life experience and understand that there are few accidents or coincidences. All is unfolding as it is meant to.

Introduction: Welcome to the Dance

As more and more people explore their individual paths, they begin reading works that grapple with the subject of destiny, such as *The Celestine Prophecy* and the writings of Thomas Moore and Frederick Buechner. The more our awareness expands and deepens, the more we begin paying attention to what we once called quirks or flukes or chance. Coincidences, as they are called, are part of a larger plan—a karma, destiny or fate—that each of us was born with.

Destiny is what unfolds for each of us every minute, every day. While it is possible, or even probable, that our destiny has been provided to us by the universe, it does not mean that we just passively let our lives play out.

Just as there are crossroads when we drive, so, too, there are choices we must make on the path that has been laid out for each of us. We can cooperate with that path and make it a wonderful journey or we can resist the path and make our own way. Sometimes the path is frightening or painful, sometimes it is bizarre and difficult to fathom.

However, if we cooperate with what the universe gives us and follow the road that beckons, we will most often find the gifts, insights and talents required to proceed with strength and courage. At the time, the destination may be far over the horizon and we are mystified and easily turned back. The ultimate purpose is not always revealed so quickly. The journey may take years.

It often happens that a new path is introduced in a way we would rather not experience, such as loss of a job, relationship or material goods. It might be a threat, a diagnosis of serious illness or an accident. It might

Introduction: Welcome to the Dance   xv

also come in the form of addiction to alcohol or drugs, bouts of depression, or obsessions with money, power or success. In coming to terms with the situation, we are challenged to question our beliefs, values and meaning of life. These introductions to a new path can be turning points that signal the start of a profound change or transformation in our lives. And change usually means discovering something new about the world . . . and ourselves.

Messengers

Fortunately, we don't have to make sense of our destiny by ourselves. We have been given messengers, mentors and teachers to help us along the way. In our selfabsorption and concerns with day-to-day living, we may have overlooked the guides among us, or we may not be aware of them or accept them in our circle of confidants.

As the old Zen saying goes, "When the student is ready, the teacher will appear."

So, too, when the universe wants to guide us, people are sent to lead the way. It is important to look, listen and be willing to be open to the messengers who will present themselves to us. They will be recognized by their charisma—or they may not be recognized at all.

Charisma is a Greek word that means "gift." Charismatic healers may be young or old, any race or from any culture. They may be rich or poor, powerful or broken. What makes them charismatic is that they have a special gift—the power to heal others.

Introduction: Welcome to the Dance

Surrounded by messengers and healers, we live in a field of inexhaustible spiritual energy. Why then is there so much pain and suffering in the world? There are many reasons: Some do not believe that the energy even exists; others are too busy to connect with it; and still others believe that spirituality is for those who regularly attend a church, or go to India to meditate. Too often, what is missed is that spirituality is the core of our everyday lives. It lives and grows in the simplest of acts but many of us are too blind or ignorant to tap into that energy.

Each of us can, in our own way, become a bearer of gifts and good tidings. During the course of the day, several ways present themselves to us to:

Hold the hand of someone who is frightened
Give a gift
Share empathy with a friend
Sit with someone who is ill
Celebrate another's good fortune
Share pleasure and laughter
Create a special meal

The list is as endless as one's imagination. What we do in our daily lives to stir the compassion, joy, relief, laughter and tears in ourselves and in others is called "spirituality in action." When we awaken to this everyday devotion, we find a profound transformation and we, too, become messengers.

This shift in focus from the mundane to the unusual, from external to internal, is another sign of changing times. For I believe we are in an era of transition—emerging from the old style of institutional spirituality to include

Introduction: Welcome to the Dance   xvii

the ordinary events that are a part of our everyday lives. It may turn out that religious institutions of the future exist mainly as a place for people to gather to share the spirituality they have found in ordinary day-to-day happenings. It is no surprise to me that *The Celestine Prophecy* spread like wildfire. Readers recognized that the adventures and possibilities presented in the book offered a framework for understanding, for giving meaning to their own personal experiences.

As we spend our days and nights fulfilling our own destinies, it is also entirely possible that something much more significant is happening. Every day, our human worlds are being transformed through spiritual evolution. Each of us is coming to our own personal perception of the spiritual world, with our own interpretation of inner evolution.

My Own Path

My own spiritual journey started many years ago and has gone through countless transitions that have given me understanding and a personal message to share. Along the way there have been unexpected changes in direction.

I feel fortunate to have grown up in a small Minnesota farming community. My early years were centered around family, school and church. As a small child, everything seemed magical. I loved the people around me, including a grandmother who taught me special enduring values early my in life. She had little money and few material goods, but she gave me a wealth of memories which remain crystal clear to this day.

xviii   *Introduction: Welcome to the Dance*

From her I learned graciousness, for she always had homemade food—like warm, sugary, cinnamon pumpkin doughnuts—for me and other guests. She taught me generosity by baking bread and making soup for the hobos who passed through town. And my grandma taught me love by opening her arms to me and everyone she knew. She radiated kindness.

Nature was also a big part of my spiritual awakening— the woods were both my outdoor cathedral and playground. I can still close my eyes and summon the sound of crunching leaves underfoot and the smell of leaves burning in the autumn.

My parents were wise and unselfish as they encouraged my friendships. Days were endless adventures and nights were party times with regular slumber parties. We laughed, learned and grew together. Life was a wonderful adventure that unfolded for me.

From my earliest memories I felt close to God. As a child, I had a brass bed with a headboard filled with decorative holes. I tied pencils on the bed post and, after being tucked in at night, plugged the pencils into the holes like the old telephone operators did. With my "divine headboard," I pretended to connect myself with God and the angels so we could talk. As a child, the connection was as real as a regular telephone conversation. For me, meditation has been a lifelong practice.

Eventually I convinced my father to convert one upstairs closet to a church where I could pray, meditate and talk to my congregation of dolls and teddy bears.

My faith was that of a child—simple, complete and largely untested. As I matured, it was questioned by the

Introduction: Welcome to the Dance xix

trauma and losses which have been sprinkled throughout my life. My first misfortune was the growing addiction by both parents to alcohol and drugs. These horrendous habits robbed me of much of my childhood; the feelings of safety and comfort were gone—replaced by the emotional desire to have my old family back again.

As I review those years, I can now see beyond the heartache and loss and recognize the gifts I received. During that time I was given the spiritual powers of strength, courage and compassion, which I call grace. The dictionary describes grace as favor, elegance, power, brilliance, joy, regeneration, blessing.

The losses of my youth were the beginning of the path I did not want to follow. Yet somehow I felt protected as I did. My faith deepened at this time and became stronger than my attachment to a church.

The trauma of my father's suicide on the Christmas Eve of his 46th year, my very painful first marriage and divorce, and my mother's addiction, added to my anguish and fulfilled the destiny I was fated to endure.

There were times I felt alone and lost. I truly loved my father and mother and I felt their loss as core pain. My marriage was devastating.

A messenger during this time gave me the word "discernment." In the dictionary I found it means to understand, to discriminate and then to choose. Knowledge and information became my passion. I devoured books and certain authors became my mentors: Anthony Padavano, Olga Worrall, Jacqueline Lair, Erich Fromm, Rollo May, Harold Kushner, J. B. Phillips and Virginia Satir.

xx   *Introduction: Welcome to the Dance*

They validated and expanded my faith with their gift of words and helped ease my pain. From the embers of the fires in my life some goodness has emerged. My three beautiful, wonderful children, a source of constant joy, have also given me numerous grandchildren. Because of these special people, I will never regret my first marriage.

As my destiny has unfolded, often taking me places I never planned or desired to go, I have learned that if I cooperate with the universe and follow the flow, I will be graced with opportunities beyond both my reasonable expectations and my wildest dreams.

It seems to happen over and over: Somehow I was given the courage to quit a job at which I was being sexually harassed; soon after, I was offered a much better job. My regret over not having gone to college as a young woman dissolved when I received my college degree as an older adult, and had the ability and energy to complete nine years of higher education.

I had a difficult and lonely time when I doggedly clung to some out-of-the-mainstream counseling theories. However, a publisher saw them, thought they had merit and invited me to write my first book. It became a bestseller. I've written many more books, several of which have also been bestsellers.

When my second marriage ended in divorce, I truly felt like a relationship failure with all the hurt, shame, guilt and loneliness a broken heart can bring. Little did I know at the time that my universe was preparing me for the personal fulfillment of a true soulmate. Looking back I realize I wasn't ready earlier. I needed emotional preparation and growth to thrive in my current relationship, which is one of my greatest sources of joy.

I was reminded one more time that my job is to follow, not control, when my recent path took me into the medical nightmare of breast cancer. When the doctors told me, I was stunned; my reaction was disbelief, anger and surprise instead of fear, panic and depression. Now I can only connect to healing, hope and learning.

My spiritual lesson and truths of the past were so instilled in me, I could not doubt that the situation would work out for the best. The presence of grace was and is so powerful in my life that I can only go forward, ready and waiting for the next step of my destiny to unfold.

Trust and Timing

Confidence and certainty have been a long time coming. For years I had read about the searching of the soul, attended workshops from Europe to Esalen, consumed books and information. Yet I remained restless until the day I realized that my spiritual hunger and satisfaction was not "out there." It was in ME—accepting, understanding and cooperating with my personal destiny—as though I had taken off a pair of dark sunglasses.

"I see," I said. "It's all crystal clear."

The message was not just for and about me; it applies equally to all souls. My losses, gifts and lessons happened for a reason—they were messages and lessons for me to hear and understand. The great figures in religion have also had experiences that have given them glimpses of light, clarity and a tangible inner peace.

xxii   *Introduction: Welcome to the Dance*

Like all people, somehow I had to find the way to live in the Spirit and in the world at the same time. The Spirit has been given hundreds of names by different peoples in different ages. Yahweh, God and Allah are just a few of the most familiar names associated with the mysterious unfolding of humanity's collective destiny, and each of our own personal prospects as well. Today this awakening is often called awareness, consciousness or spirituality.

Millions of men and women are trying to fathom the work of the divine as they play out their fate. This quote from Anthony Padavano captures the frustration that we can feel from the push and pull we experience when we try to come to grips with where we're going and why.

We wait for life to keep unfolding. We try to understand its meaning, year by year, experience by experience. We may control our actions, speed up our movements, resist schedules, but in truth life will unfold at its own pace.

Many of us stumble down the path of spiritual development when we stop trusting our internal guide—when we stop listening to the lessons taught by our own experiences—and look for a guru to answer our questions for us. While it's important to be open to messengers and angels, it is also important to understand and discern our own rhythm in the life of the Spirit.

When we connect to our own framework and listen to our messengers and angels, we can see that everything is happening in God's good time. We must trust that we are moving in step with our divine partner. And when we accept that we don't know where the next step will lead, but are still able to put our feet forward with confidence, then we will no longer stumble. We will be free to follow our path and dance with our destiny.

Sam Keen, the author, once said something that has stayed with me: "I'll only believe in a God who can dance."

The idea of seeing the unfolding of destiny as a dance with God delights me, for dancing is all about movement and expression—making the Spirit that moves us visible in the world.

On a daily basis I am deeply grateful that I have God as my partner and I welcome you to join me as we celebrate and dance with destiny.

PART ONE

LEARNING TO DANCE

Dancing Lessons:
The Basics

---

*Peculiar travel suggestions are
dancing lessons from God.*

—Kurt Vonnegut Jr.

Each of us is learning to dance with our own personal destiny. Every dance is unique; there are as many different variations as there are people. For some, destiny may unfold in bold dramatic steps like a tango; for others it may play out in the measured paces of a minuet. But for all of us, there is a dance, even when we refuse to acknowledge it and act like wallflowers, watching from the side.

While the forms may differ, there are some dance steps that are common elements:

We move through space and time
We perform in a particular rhythm

3

4   *Learning to Dance*

We strive to achieve a particular look
We express a feeling or tell a story

The myriad dances of destiny also share some common elements. The first of these shared traits is that every dance of destiny occurs under divine protection.

DIVINE PROTECTION

*Sometimes I go about pitying
myself and all the time I am being carried
on great winds across the sky.*

—Ojibway Touchstones

 n times of great trauma, as well as in times of joyous celebration, we wonder and marvel at what has befallen us. How did this happen? On a day-to-day basis, it seems like we are captains of our ships, steering where we want to go and hoping for smooth sailing.

Yet if we look back at the events of our life, we can see patterns and reasons for events. If you are reading this, you can be sure that the circumstances that brought you to the point of picking up this book at this time were destined by means beyond your control.

You were born a helpless little child. Along the way you were nurtured and protected until you could care for yourself. Then you took on the task of getting yourself to where you are today. Actually, you and your God, or divine presence, brought you to this point. We might call the forces that watched over you "divine protection."

As you look back over your life, you will be able to identify times when you were divinely protected. Some may be more obvious than others, but the fact remains the protection is always there, even when we don't acknowledge it. As we reframe our history and experiences in this way, we can more easily trust that our present and future experiences are for our benefit. These events that I experienced will illustrate what I mean.

Topped-Off Travel

When I was a child my family vacationed in Florida. Before we left our Minnesota town on an old two-lane highway, my dad would stop and pick up a six-pack of Coca-Cola and another of Orange Crush. My brother, sister and I would "drink the tops off" the bottles of soda. For us that meant drinking the top half of the bottle. My dad would then fill up the Coke bottles with rum for himself and the Orange Crush with vodka for my mom. We'd take off at 85 miles per hour and cruise all the way to Florida.

We drove straight through, stopping only for gas, soda, food and liquor. Not once were we involved in a traffic accident, despite two intoxicated drivers tearing across the country at dangerous speeds. That's no way to travel, but I believe divine protection got us there and back safely.

The Right Side of Town

One hot, summer night I was coming home from a teaching class at the University of Minnesota about 10:30 P.M. I was tired and decided to take a short cut through a part of town known for its high crime rate. About halfway through this fairly dangerous district, a tire on my car blew. I could hear the rim of the wheel clanking on the highway. It was clear I was not going to be able to go on so I got out of the car, despite my fear.

After walking down a few dark blocks, I saw a faint light coming from the porch of a large house. Gathering my courage, I headed for it and, after climbing the steps, peeked inside a screen door. Inside were a group of tough-looking men. My first instinct was to run. But to where?

Finally I knocked. A burly man answered and listened as I explained my plight. He interrupted by asking if I was "the alcohol lady." He then produced one of my books with my picture on it. I had stumbled into a local AA meeting. The whole group trudged down the hill, fixed my tire, shared the serenity prayer with me and I was on my way.

Instead of being on the *wrong* side of town, I was on the *right* side.

Red Rose of Texas

After years of personal and professional life in Minnesota, several developments indicated to me that it was time to leave. It was during the winter of 1982-83 that I decided to make a change. Having secured a good job in Texas, I sold my home, left my family, friends and career, and headed south on a cold December day.

I drove my small gray Honda dressed in a gray snowsuit with a red knit hat and red down-lined cowboy boots. A few hours into the three-day drive, I found myself in the thick of a snowstorm. By the time I neared the Texas border after two days of treacherous driving on ice, I had grown tense and vulnerable.

I felt personally lonely and professionally isolated. The tears began to flow. After about two hours of crying and driving, I prayed.

"Dear God, I feel so alone and so unsure. If you are there, please give me a sign."

A short while later I saw a roadside diner and decided to stop and take a break.

As I entered, I picked up a magazine that looked interesting, then sat down in a booth. When the waitress came over, the first thing she said was, "You must be the Red Rose." Puzzled, I asked her to explain.

"The truck drivers are all talking about the Red Rose," she said. "Some lady left Minnesota in a small gray Honda in the middle of a snowstorm, and they've been watching out for her from Minnesota to the Texas border. They've followed her on their CB radios to make sure she was okay. I see you've made it, and I'll let them know."

My tears began to flow again, this time from relief and gratitude. I felt watched over and protected. The sign had

Divine Protection   9

been given to me—someone did care. As I ate, I opened the magazine to which I was drawn. An article entitled "Families of Alcoholics Recover" caught my eye. The article began "Sharon Wegscheider, in her work, reports . . ." I could not remember giving an interview to this particular magazine, and yet here was an article about my work. The tears gave way to a smile.

Spiritual Truths

*If you would learn the secret of right relations,
look only for the divine in people and
things, and leave the rest to God.*

—J. Allen Boone

ertain spiritual lessons and central truths are revealed through history time and again via different messengers and events. I believe they include the following:

1. *There is a force that guides us, protects us and introduces us to our path and each other.* This power offers us divine protection and direction through the process of miracles.
2. *God answers prayers by sending people known as messengers or angels.* Sometimes angels have wings and can take us to spiritual heights but more often

12   *Learning to Dance*

they have feet and live in our midst. You may have known several and you may have become one.

3. *Transformation does not happen all at once, it occurs little by little.* When we can go neither forward nor back, we are coming upon a time of transformation. A path will present itself.

4. *Discernment is the spiritual gift that propels us to follow our path.* We all have the ability to make ongoing decisions about work, relationships, lifestyle and direction. Those who do live in the "now" and believe every day presents a possible adventure.

5. *Losses can become lessons.* Embracing our losses leads to feelings and awareness that offer new paths to follow.

6. *Turning points are spiritual interruptions in our state of well-being that tell us destiny is taking us to another place.* So often we wonder why certain things happen to us. A call, a visit, an illness or an accident can feel like an interruption when it is really a wake-up call.

7. *We can be guided through storytelling*—what we hear from friends, what we read in books, what we watch and hear through the media and Internet. Instructions that serve as a "contemporary catechism" come to us through many messengers and channels of communication.

8. *Inner spiritual peace does not come from being spared pain and suffering.* Instead it comes from knowing how to accept, surrender and be able to use the pain and suffering to help us fulfill our destiny by being able to see the large picture of life.

One Step at a Time

The art of living lies not in eliminating, but in growing with trouble.

—Bernard M. Baruch

ew people learn a particular dance, especially a difficult one, all at once. They learn the movements one step at a time. It's the same with the dance of destiny. And like dances we learn with the body, this dance with the Spirit only begins to make sense when we know all the moves.

The more we know and trust the dance, the easier it becomes to cooperate with the universe and fulfill our destiny. Dancing becomes a pleasure, something we want to share with and teach to others. This is another one of those things that is easier said than done because life sometimes seems as though it's one problem after another.

I once heard someone say that "true spirituality is living life forward but understanding it backwards."

As we look, we can make sense of what has happened in our lives. We review our birth, childhood, adolescence and adult life experiences. As we ponder how they all fit together, we begin to get a picture of our purpose.

Being a busy and productive sort of person, I plan ahead and organize my calendar, trying to keep my life under control. But so often my plans are changed by events beyond my command.

When roadblocks are put on my path, I am sometimes forced to find another way. Sometimes they are merely obstacles. Today, as I look back, I can see they were helping the journey go just the way it needed to go. I arrived at my intended destination in spite of myself.

Our destiny unfolds from the inside out, like a flower. Just as each bloom is a unique example of perfect color and design created by the universe, so are we. Can you imagine the foolishness and waste of prying open a rose?

I Asked

I asked God for strength that I might achieve;
I was made weak that I might humbly learn to obey.

I asked for help that I might do great things;
I was given infirmity that I might do better things.

I asked for riches that I might be happy;
I was given poverty that I might be wise.

I asked for power that I might have the praise of men;
I was given weakness that I might feel the need of God.

I asked for all things that I might enjoy life;
I was given life that I might enjoy all things.

I asked for a vision that I might control my future;
I was given awareness that I might be grateful now.

I got nothing I asked for but everything I had hoped for.
Almost in spite of myself my unspoken prayers were answered.

I am among all people most richly blessed.

Just as we assume that the rose will unfold just as it should, we can assume that the rest of the world is unfolding according to God's plan, even though God often likes to work in strange ways. The following parable illustrates the mysterious ways of the Spirit.

"When God wants an important thing done in His world, or a wrong righted, He acts in a roundabout fashion. He never lets loose with lightning or stirs up earthquakes. Instead, He has a baby born."

From this time-honored tale, we have a hint of meaning for our own lives. Each of us is a baby, born to a life of challenge, choices and transformation. Each of us must remain open to the Spirit—to the challenges of spiritual transformation that come one step at a time.

The experience of a hectic spiritual quest can leave one feeling empty. Rushing from guru to guru takes so much energy that it's likely one will miss the unwrapping of one's present of life. Fatigue and desperation are not spiritual gifts. Blooming where you are planted, remaining curious about your own path and maintaining an attentive self-awareness are the steps to a series of discoveries. Our destiny is revealed in stages and comes to us in turning points—miracles large and small.

Out of the Mouths of Babes
(Paulette's Story)

I was widowed in my early twenties when my daughter was just over a year old. The loss of my husband had a great effect on me. A few years later I was involved in a relationship that was ending. All of my old feelings of loss and abandonment came flooding back.

My little girl could sense something was wrong. She asked me why I was so sad. When I said my partner was not going to be with us anymore and I was unhappy and lonely, she put her head on my lap.

With wide, wise eyes, she looked up and said, "That's okay, Mom, you've still got me."

Immediately, I felt a surge of peace and love. My little angel had put my perspective back into focus. There had been a loss but my life was still full of love and meaning.

A Loving Spoonful
(Patty's Story)

In 1956 I was an 18-year-old pregnant, insecure woman. I felt like a little girl inside and at the time marriage seemed the only solution to my problems. The pregnancy was kept secret as I prepared for a modest wedding.

One Step at a Time   17

For many years while growing up, the public library was my safe haven. Bertha, the librarian, always treated me with respect and appeared interested when I shared parts of my life with her. When I told her of my upcoming wedding, she congratulated me warmly and later presented me with a beautiful silver serving spoon.

But Bertha never really knew what else she gave me along with the gift. Her endless encouragement was the true present. "You can do anything you want," she'd tell me. "You are capable and you are worthy of beautiful things."

Bertha was one of the first angels in my life.

MIRACLES

*The sign must come like the dawn.
You cannot see its arrival, but
know when it's there.*

—Diane Wakoski

he dictionary says miracles are events that appear to be unexplainable by laws of nature so they are held to be acts of God. For many of us the age of miracles is long past. However, for those who trust the dance with the Spirit, miracles happen every day.

When we reframe our personal development and view it through the lens of the Spirit, we begin to see the miracles we have already experienced. Many of what we once called coincidences are now revealed to be miracles.

When we open our eyes and hearts, we discover that every event has significance and contains answers that pertain to our unasked questions. Particular people cross our paths for a purpose and carry messages for us. Even dreams can tell us about parts of our lives that need to be illuminated. Our job is to stay awake and aware, alert to the miracles around us.

As we recognize the marvelous things in our lives, we begin to be aware of a mystical quality and feel a connection with events and people. There is a sensation of euphoria, a sense of warmth, security and comfort that comes from knowing we are connected—that we are on our intended path. Living in the miracle of being awake to our spiritual connection becomes a lifestyle to strive for.

There is a gift of energy released that we receive from these spiritual events and connections. This energy is called grace; it can come in many forms. A few of the words we use to describe it include:

trust	affirmation
patience	healing
strength	perseverance
courage	wisdom

One of the most delightful discoveries in learning how to dance with destiny is that the more a person dances, or cooperates with the Spirit, the more grace is received and experienced and, thus, more miracles happen.

Like many good things in life, it's not easy to cooperate with destiny. We come from a culture and a tradition that values control, domination, achievement and accumulation. The dark side is the alienation, violence, loss

Miracles   21

and emptiness we see manifested daily in disrespect for
human life, danger to women and children, hopelessness
and the rigid judgments of hate-groups.

In recent years my counseling work has also taught me
about the emptiness of many spoiled children and hol-
lowness of the privileged section of society—people who
are no longer satisfied with continuous travel, sport and
meaningless acquisitions. My friend Mel Buchholtz
speaks eloquently about the plight of the "worried well."
The success of books like *Acts of Kindness*, *Life's Little
Instruction Book* and *Love, Medicine & Miracles* shows us
that something is needed to fill the loneliness and emptiness that pervades this affluent part of society.

The recognition of miracles and the infusion of grace
can become new anchors to help fill the void of insin-
cerity. Understanding how life works will guide us and
enable us to take the risks that will connect us more
deeply with each other and with the Spirit.

There was a time when the words "miracle" and
"grace" were the exclusive province of theologians,
churches and scholars. Now, however, we see miracles
in everyday life and experience grace with regularity.

Miracles happen when one looks honestly at a chaotic
marriage, at personal fragmentation, at conflict between
parent and child, at addiction to chemicals and dependency behavior, and one begins to make changes to
resolve these issues.

Miracles need not be accompanied by a thunder-
bolt from heaven or a cataclysmic event. A spiritual
sensation can take place under the most mundane
circumstances.

A mother and daughter look into each others' eyes and admit their sorrow and pain over misunderstandings that happened years ago. They hold each other and forgive each other.

A father and son both accept their addiction to alcohol and drugs and go through treatment together.

Spouses forgive each other for past hurts and start over with fresh hearts.

A teenage girl feels her first spiritual awakening because someone really listens to her pain.

A man weeps and finally accepts the death of his father which occurred many years before.

A woman looks at herself in the mirror and likes what she sees—forgiving herself for her addictive illness.

Miracles happen wherever and whenever people admit their chaos and pain and move outside themselves to search for healing. Recognizing that miracles are the stuff of everyday life is a human endeavor. Author and counselor Roxy Lerner put it this way: "If we live too much in the spiritual plane, we become no earthly good."

The Fire
(Marty's Miracle)

The night my heating pad malfunctioned and set fire to the dust ruffle of my bed, I was awakened by a clear and calm voice calling my name.

"Marty," it said. A moment later it called louder, more insistently, "Marty!"

There was nobody around when I was jerked awake, feeling a burning sensation in my hand. I had taken this same heating pad off my daughter's pillow hours earlier when she complained that it was too hot.

I quickly extinguished the small flame with a spritzer bottle of water and sleepily dozed off again. I must have heard the voice again because I was jerked awake remembering that dry sparks from an electrical fire can ignite a mattress without any visible sign. Had I just read that somewhere?

I decided not to call the fire department. I had only recently finished cleaning up the flooding in my lower floor due to excess rain and a failed sump pump and I wasn't going to risk having my carpet flooded again.

I called a neighbor who, with no questions asked, came right over. Together we hauled the smoldering mattress and boxspring outside into a light drizzle. Then I went back inside to wait until daylight. As I checked on my sleeping daughters and felt relief that they had been spared, I realized that it had to have been a guardian angel's voice awakening me and staying with me until the danger was past.

The Gift of Tears
(Bill's Miracle)

It might sound strange to say that a person who has just attempted suicide could be an angel. But that person changed my life by a single act of desperation. The person who gave me the gift was no stranger, she was my daughter.

I was raised in a family with great material comforts but little human warmth. My parents were middle-aged when I was born and their marriage was not a happy one. My father never displayed affection or explained emotion. My mother drank quietly to hide her own unhappiness. With this kind of modeling, I grew up unable to feel. I also inherited the family legacy of alcoholism.

As an adult I had a great desire to build a better family but I lacked the experience to go about it. So I repeated the pattern of distance and frozen emotions. I found sobriety from my own alcohol problems when my children were teenagers. I learned how to think straight without medicating myself and how to be spiritual in AA. But still I did not know how to feel.

Even therapy couldn't help. The change came when my daughter was 16. The ravages of alcohol and a frozen family crashed down on her at a time when she should have been carefree and happy. She took an overdose of pills; a friend got her to the hospital just in time.

Amazingly, I became the model of efficiency. I found a treatment center, drove her to the airport, flew with her to the center and checked her in. I was a calm and concerned parent.

It was on the way home that the miracle occurred. Somehow my reserve broke on the last leg of the journey and I began to pray.

"God, why did this have to happen to her?" I asked. The weight of loss was unbearable. Everyone I loved had been affected by the pain caused by a lack of emotional support handed down for generations. This time it had struck my flesh and blood. Tears began to fall, the deep freeze began to thaw. I wept for a lifetime of pain and grief.

Miracles   25

Since that time I can cry at any appropriate time. All the feelings of anger, sadness and joy are fully present every moment of the day and night. I am able to share those deepest parts of me with the people I love.

When my daughter married, all those emotions came to the surface. As I escorted her down the aisle, I cried with both sadness at her leaving the family and gratitude for the gift she had given me.

Lost and Found

*The years forever fashion new dreams
when old ones go. God pity the
one-dream man.*

—Robert Goddard

he dance with destiny is never static. Sometimes our favorite steps, or even whole routines, must be given up. But for every loss, something new is added to our repertoire.

Many times in my life I experienced devastating losses. Anger, hurt, fear and helplessness echoed within me. After a while I learned to trust the process and began to see the loss as part of the bigger picture, the unfolding of my future.

When I Lost . . .	I Found . . .
My father at an early age.	Confidence to care for myself.
Friends when I divorced.	New relationships.
My ability to be strong.	The ability to accept support.
Friends to addiction and co-dependency.	Ability to set boundaries for myself.
My job because of my convictions.	A whole new field to work in with the best professionals.
An early marriage.	My soulmate.
My health.	A commitment to self-care.

When we accept the give and take of losing and finding, we learn that life is not about control but about watching and feeling the mystery unfold. It has been said that part of living a full life is learning to let go of things: the total security of nursing at a mother's breast, the safety and comfort of home, the vitality and beauty of youth, the status of achievement, physical health and strength and eventually, life itself.

Today, as we understand the chaos of the past, we can take comfort in knowing that everything has happened as it should. Even more reassuring, we can believe that it will continue to do so in the future, enabling us to lose our fear and find greater trust.

Lost and Found

She Offered Me Hope
(Kathy's Story)

I met her only once in my life—at a conference for adult children of alcoholics. What she said touched me deeply.

I learned that because of my denial about the family history of drinking that my husband and I shared, our children had been placed at risk. When I realized this I began to cry.

The wonderful lady sitting next to me told me her story and offered me renewed hope. She told of a place I could go for help. The next day my recovery started.

This is my chance to thank Billie Odell. Thank you from the bottom of my heart.

Love Power
(Pete's Story)

I was at the lowest point in my life. My wife and year-old daughter had moved with me to Michigan where I was appointed program director at a mental health agency.

While I had been fairly successful in managing three to four people, I was totally inept at managing 18, and was not up to the task of developing policies and procedures. The State of Michigan was in financial distress. The reports about my job performance were poor and my staff was complaining bitterly about my lack of management skills. It was no wonder that I was laid off. I hit rock bottom.

My wife did not leave me despite the clear failure I had

become. I couldn't understand why she stuck with me even though it looked as though I would be unable to provide for my family. I admit I wasn't much of a partner in those days.

Her love and loyalty taught me more about commitment that I had learned in the 30 years previous. I learned that I could be loved for me and not for what I did or could provide. This is the greatest story I can share in celebration of the 20 years we have now spent together.

Prayer and Meditation

> *Prayer is a key to the source of power. Meditation and contemplation may be looked upon as keys used by a healer to open doors to spiritual knowledge to turn on the healing current, and to bring into focus that which God is ready to reveal through the use of spiritual gifts.*
>
> —Olga Worrall

ancers rigorously train their bodies and minds, knowing that constant training produces the most expressive and most enchanting movements. Without this care and attention to their physical bodies, they would not have the energy to make the dance come alive.

The dance of destiny requires no less dedication and energy. The spiritual force that makes the dance alive and vibrant in our everyday lives is connected to prayer and meditation which allow us to find the calm center amid the stress and chaos. In the quiet stillness of worship we can feel the unfolding of our personal destiny by giving the soul time to reveal itself. We practice stillness to expand our awareness and deepen our consciousness so ideas, answers and possibilities are revealed.

These visions give us the direction we need to move in harmony with the universe. When we do not move with the universe, our path seems difficult and filled with obstacles. At the very heart of all creation is an infinitely orchestrated, fully comprehended consciousness which has made each of us unique.

The Prayer Table
(Sharon's Tale)

Several years ago a woman I respected told me about the prayer corner in her bedroom. It had a rocking chair and a glass-topped table on which she placed a tape recorder, tapes and books for meditation. Each morning after reading a passage, she would look at the names of people she knew that were stuck to the table top with Post-it notes.

I decided to do the same thing. Now my husband and I both have rocking chairs, tapes, books and sticky notes on which we place the names of our family members and friends. Morning meditation has become a treasured part of our day, thanks to a lovely woman who shared the secret of sending messages to loved ones.

The Voice of a Guardian Angel
(Shirley's Tale)

When my husband died I couldn't believe the number of "angels" who entered my life in various ways. The most vivid and strongest presence I felt was on my way home from a little mountain town located 200 miles from my home in Tucson, Arizona.

The road is well-paved but very curvy and in some places narrow and steep. I had driven it several times during the summer but on this particular occasion I had loaded my station wagon with the contents of the cabin where we had spent so many happy years. It was sold and I was carting home the goods without an inch of space to spare in the car.

It was a sad and lonely time. I was absolutely drained, emotionally and physically. About halfway home I had the feeling that I just could not make it any further when I sensed a presence in the car with me.

A voice said, "Come on, Shirl, you can make it."

Immediately I felt lifted in body and spirit. Two hours later I pulled into my carport safe and sound. As I sat there grateful to be home, I heard that voice again and sensed the Spirit around me. This time it said, "Good job. You'll be okay now."

I guess I truly have a guardian angel after all.

The God Box
(Patty's Story)

In 1990 I was in the middle of my counselor training program when my mother took ill and had to be placed in a nursing home. The number of trips from my home to her apartment on the Minnesota-Iowa border used up most of my carefully budgeted money.

One of the residents of the nursing home spoke about his "God Box." He said he wrote his troubles on a small piece of paper and placed them in the box when he went to bed. He said he trusted God would take care of his concerns.

When I got home I looked for a box but couldn't find one so I used my desk drawer instead. I wrote "financial worries" on a small scrap, put it in the drawer and tumbled into bed. Within two days I had completely forgotten about the God Box but when I opened my mail, I was instantly reminded. One of the envelopes contained a check for a thousand dollars. It was the scholarship I had applied for months ago.

THE ONE AND ONLY

*I have said that the soul is
not more than the body, and I have said
that the body is not more than the soul,
and nothing, not God, is greater
to one than one's self is.*

—Walt Whitman

here never has been, nor will there ever be, another you. You have your own fingerprints and you are truly "one of a kind." Your destiny is unique and so is your dance with it.

Only *you* can fulfill the destiny that is planned for you. Your world and surroundings are created only for you, talents and gifts have been given to you, you are part of a master purpose for the world. Only you have the opportunity to contribute to this purpose. By flowing with the plans of the universe, you have the chance to discover the greatest excitement and fulfillment possible. You have been given the power to make choices about the special you. When you choose to accept your destiny, rewards will be plentiful and when you are finished in this world, it will be a better place because of you.

Gratitude
(Author Virginia Satir's Tribute to Her Friends, Colleagues and Family)

I send you love. Please support me in
my passage to a new life.
I have no other way to thank you than this.
You have all played a significant part
in my development of loving.
As a result, my life has been rich and full so
I leave feeling very grateful.
—Virginia Satir

Single Mom's Reward
(Amy's Story)

The United Way has a Community Day Care in our area. One Saturday we gathered at the early hour of seven in the morning to give back to the community. I had signed up my eight-year-old son and myself to help fix a neighborhood center used as a meeting place for mentally challenged children.

We dragged ourselves over there, cleaned, painted, washed, dug ditches and gardened all day. I don't think we ever worked so hard. Some of the kids from the center helped us and Austin had his first experience with people who were different from him but who were loving and caring.

It felt good helping out and introducing my son to the rewards of serving others. We both felt a deep sense of satisfaction and we both agreed to sign up again next year.

The Healing Touch
(Kathy Remembers)

There wasn't much affection in my home when I was growing up. There was even less touching. The exception was my paternal grandma—a huge woman with the biggest and best lap I've ever seen.

She was always available. I don't ever remember her saying "I'm too busy" or "get off." Her lap was big enough to hold me and my sister at the same time.

There are many stories of how mean she could be to her own offspring but to me she was an angel. She taught me that touching is important and can heal even the deepest emotional wounds.

DISCERNMENT

*Being faithful is not about clinging
to first commitments or relationships that are dead.
Faithfulness is about clinging to the life force
within each of us and finding the courage to choose
life over death—no matter the cost.*

—Anthony Padavano

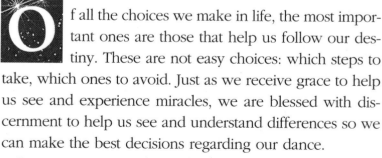f all the choices we make in life, the most important ones are those that help us follow our destiny. These are not easy choices: which steps to take, which ones to avoid. Just as we receive grace to help us see and experience miracles, we are blessed with discernment to help us see and understand differences so we can make the best decisions regarding our dance.

Discernment goes by many names: sharpness, keenness, perception, mental vision, insight. Whatever the name, it is a spiritual gift that places us on our path and keeps us true to the direction it is following.

When we first enter into the process of transformation, we will be faced with choices that are not too difficult, just as we might learn simpler dances before advancing to more difficult ones. The early choices may be between something less satisfying and something more satisfying. That's not too hard; obviously we would choose something more satisfying.

As the process continues, however, the chores become more difficult. Even if we have something that is "more satisfying," we will at some point want to choose something even better. To do so, we must give up that which is only "more satisfying." Then we have even better things. If we choose to have the very best, we will eventually have to give up very good things in order to achieve the best. Eventually all our choices will be between the best and the best: That's living a very fulfilled life with lots of choices.

Discernment is being able to let go of something in order to have the clarity and the energy to grasp something new—whether it is a creation, a relationship, a career or even a new environment. Be aware that decision-making requires action and assertiveness.

Sometimes it doesn't even matter if it's a good or bad decision. All that matters is that someone makes a decision to do something different. One can learn from success or failure, so action, any action, is the positive step.

Just as movement is the essence of a dance of the body, faith gives us the strength to take spiritual leaps. Even if we fail, we have communicated our willingness to be part of the dance which brings us to a new level of grace and the serenity to await the new steps and opportunities that will surely follow our act of faith.

You Get Back What You Give Away
(Dr. Ray's Story)

An elderly patient of mine suffered from heart disease, arthritis, hearing loss and was nearly blind. I felt bad that there was little I could do for her.

Every year she'd give me a birthday card with $5. When I told her she didn't have to do this she got very serious and said that my compassion to her was a blessing she had received. She added that she'd be hurt if I refused her gift.

I received a lot more than cards and money from that angel of a woman. She showed me grace, humility and respect. I learned you do get back that which you give away.

Butterflies Lift Spirits
(Libby's Tale)

My grandmother was an angel to her grandchildren. I felt truly loved and accepted by her.

She had an intense love for butterflies and red cardinals. Since her death I have had several incidents in which I was visited by these interesting creatures. Three years ago during a 2,000-mile cross-country move, I was almost at my destination when I found myself overwhelmed by fear. As I thought about turning around and heading back to familiar territory, my car was surrounded by butterflies. These bright, yellow-winged angels stayed with me for about 10 minutes as I drove. Their presence calmed my jitters and made me ready to face the many challenges that lay ahead.

The Colonel
(Sharon's Memory)

As a young family therapist years ago, my dream was to study with one of the masters. Her name was Virginia Satir. As a single parent and full-time student, money was scarce. After much investigating I found Virginia was presenting a workshop in Canada. Since I lived in Minnesota, getting there seemed impossible.

At the time I volunteered my counseling skills at a halfway house for war veterans. One of the men was known as The Colonel; he became a special friend, a kind of grandpa to my children. One night after he had come for dinner, I was telling him of my plight. He listened carefully but didn't say much.

Later, as I was straightening up the living room I noticed a piece of paper between the couch cushions. I opened it and out fell a check for $400. A note inside read, "Go study. Take what you have learned and pass it on."

My airfare to Canada was $388. The trip began a lifelong relationship between Virginia and me. We made a movie together and became close personal friends. My angel, The Colonel, made it all possible.

BORN TO DANCE

There is one more element that each of our individual dances with destiny shares—it is something we were all born to do. It is our birthright and one of life's true delights.

We must dare to believe that the world really exists for us. That is why the dance of destiny takes place under divine protection, why it is revealed to us one step at a time and why miracles are the stuff of everyday life. It is why when learning the dance we begin to see loss as the step just before gain. It is why we can tap into abundant spiritual energy through prayer and meditation and to use discernment to make the choices that enable us to fulfill our unique destiny.

Once we begin to dance with destiny, we enter into a process of transformation that never really ends. It is our unique creation, never to be repeated and always to be acknowledged for the miracle it is.

PART TWO

TRANSFORMATIONS OF THE HEART

Becoming One with Our Destiny

*To turn, turn will be our delight
'til by turning we come 'round right . . .*

—from "Simple Gifts," a Shaker song

ach one of us has a singular destiny and a unique path to travel. This can be both frightening and freeing. It frightens us because there is no road map; our individual journeys have never been undertaken before. It is freeing because we discover our uniqueness when we follow our hearts and minds in the Spirit of faith.

While there is no map, there are tales from other travelers that give us hope and knowledge. Their stories can inspire us, deepen our faith and help us reframe our own experience. If they have done it, often against daunting odds, we can, too.

There is tremendous power in sharing stories, for out of our common experience comes a collective wisdom to guide each of us. In many faiths these stories illustrate the tragedies and triumphs of becoming fully human; they play an integral part of holy scriptures. Each generation discovers these timeless truths of transformation in their own experience.

I am grateful for the following stories which are shared by fellow travelers I have met along my path. I hope they will inspire you as they have me and help you find sure footing in your own dance with destiny.

One Healer, One Story
(Harry Owens)

It has been said that opportunity comes only to those who can see it. Just before dawn on a mild day in May 1958, I was headed out of St. Louis on what was then called Highway 66. I had finished my freshman year at college and was going home to Los Angeles.

I had a strong sense of anticipation, for I would soon be in northern Arizona where, as a child, I had spent many summers on my aunt and uncle's sheep ranch. After my uncle had retired and sold the ranch, I had worked summers at Camp Tocaloma, a boys' and girls' camp just south of Flagstaff. This part of Arizona still felt like home to me, and I planned to spend one night at the camp.

I knew there would be no campers yet and that the camp would be deserted at that time of year. Nevertheless, I headed down a wretched old logging road which led me

Becoming One with Our Destiny 49

to Camp Tocaloma. After a simple dinner I settled down for bed on the porch of the main cabin and watched the sunset and night stars emerge in the purple sky. The next morning I strolled down to the lake. There were no new footprints so I figured I was probably the first person to visit it that particular summer. The sun was just clearing the horizon when I got to the water's edge so I started around the northeast side to look for a good spot to sit down.

The lake was small, probably less than 10 acres when full. About halfway around the lake I came to an old, burned-out tree stump; it had been there for as long as I could remember. I sat and looked at the rising sun for awhile and thought about that old stump. I figured it had been struck by lightning, a fairly common thing in these mountains.

"That's right," said a calm voice right behind me. I lost my balance as I spun around to see who it was. Sitting cross-legged on a rock just three feet behind me was an old man with a big smile on his face and a mischievous gleam in his eyes.

"I didn't hear you walk up behind me so you startled me a bit," I said, picking myself off the ground. He was dressed in worn jeans, a dark shirt, a denim jacket and leather moccasins. He wore a cowboy hat with an Arizona crown, similar to mine. His hair was white and short; his tanned, deeply lined face was distinctly Native American. He had to be old but he appeared ageless.

"I didn't mean to startle you," he said in a gentle voice. "You're here early this year. I saw you, Butch, and I wanted to visit with you."

How did he know my nickname? "Butch" was what I had been called around here. I scoured my memory but I couldn't recognize him; I was fairly sure that I never met him before.

"I'm sorry, sir, but I don't know your name. Have we met before?"

"Not officially, Butch, but I've had my eye on you, so to speak, for some time. You can call me Lodehmah," he said, pronouncing it low-day-mah.

"Isn't that an Indian word that means peace or greeting?"

"In more recent times that's about right," he replied. "But once, a long time ago, it meant healer."

I wasn't frightened, for his manner was so gentle, but I was feeling awkward and confused. I guess it showed.

"You were right, you know; that burned stump had been a tree that was struck by lightning."

I turned my head away from Lodehmah and glanced at the burned stump. Then I remembered that I had been looking at the stump and figuring that it had been a lightning-struck tree when Lodehmah first spoke to me.

"Lodehmah," I said, "how did you know that was what I was thinking?"

He grinned. "I just knew. There are other things that I know and I would like to tell you about them. Would you like to hear the story of that tree?"

I was more perplexed than ever, but also fascinated and honored that he was taking time to visit with me.

"Yes, I'd like to hear the story," I said. "But, Lodehmah, a little earlier you said I was here early this summer. Have you seen me here over past summers?"

He paused slightly and his voice took on a quieter, serious tone. "Yes, I've seen you here in the past summers but you didn't see me. And I knew you would be here today, which is why I'm here now. But we're getting a bit ahead of ourselves so let's start with the story of the tree."

He explained that long ago, before the white man or the

Hopi, Navaho and Apache, there lived a different people who were peaceful and contented. Eventually discord arose among them. Then powerful healers emerged who struggled to bring the different factions together for a meeting in this very place.

The meeting was in progress when once again fighting broke out among the group's leaders. In the midst of a heated argument, a bolt of lightning came from a clear blue sky and struck this tree. It burst into flame and burned until only that stump remained.

The people and their leaders were terribly frightened. They realized that this lightning was a sign and that the Great Spirit was showing disfavor with them. The people asked what could be done to win back the favor of the Great Spirit.

The healers told the people that they should return to the valleys and work to bring harmony to their lives; to bring back a balance in spirit, mind and body; to look once again to the value of life, all life, as the Great Spirit has given it to them.

"Furthermore," he said, "the healers would also return to the valleys with the people to help show them the healing pathways," said Lodehmah. "All the healers except one, that is. One was chosen to remain behind to tell this story, to help prepare other healers as time would go by. The burned tree would remain as a symbol of what had taken place that day.

"No sooner had the healers finished handing down the directive than a large blue heron flew over the meadow, slowly circled over the people, and flew off to the east end of the meadow and out of sight. The people took this as a good omen from the Great Spirit. For until that moment no such bird had ever been sighted in this area.

"To this day, as you have seen, Butch, a blue heron can be seen at times flying low over the meadow and lake."

He was right. I had often seen a graceful blue heron fly over the meadow. I pondered over Lodehmah's story, not knowing what to say.

Finally I broke the silence by asking, "Lodehmah, how could this burnt stump have lasted all that time? It must have been here for centuries."

"Yes," he said, "it has been a long time. Sometimes nature can delay or alter a certain course if there is a good reason and a special directive. Who knows in this case?" He smiled. "Butch, there is one more story I need to tell you." His voice once again became subdued and serious.

"This story concerns you and it's the real reason why I am here this morning. You see, you have been chosen to be a healer."

"You mean I'm supposed to be a doctor or something like that?"

He smiled and said, "Medicine, or being a physician, is but one pathway a healer may take. As a healer your job will be to help others restore their balance in spirit, mind and body—to help them to heal themselves."

He paused slightly, "Your exact pathway will be clearer as time goes by."

As he sat cross-legged, he reached down and picked up a handful of small rocks and pebbles and began to place them on the ground in the design of a circle.

"Time passes by and has an element of repetition. The stones in this circle represent special healers down through time since the day that tree was struck by lightning." He had all but finished completing the circle with the rocks and held just one small stone in his hand. "Only one is needed to complete the circle in this time frame. Then a new era can begin."

With that, he reached across and placed the stone in my hand.

"It is the time of your choosing, Butch. All healers have wounds themselves that need to be healed and these wounds will accumulate over time. Don't be dismayed by your life circumstances. You can come back here to this spot and I'll help you. Eventually a healer is healed. Once that transformation takes place you will be able to move on. You will know when that time comes, so do not be concerned about it now."

Then he stood and turned slightly. We had been facing in an easterly direction toward the far end of the meadow. Lodehmah now looked out across the lake toward the southwest, cupped his hands around his mouth, and shouted "Lo-deh-mah!"

A split second later one of the loudest and clearest echoes I've ever heard bounced back at us. I had been at this camp for six summers and had been all over those hills and around that lake and had never known that echo phenomenon to exist. I said as much to Lodehmah.

He smiled. "There is now. And it will remain here for you and others. As I said, initially, you can come back here anytime and call me. You probably won't see me, but I'll be able to help. Eventually you will learn that the answers to your questions lie within your heart and you will no longer need to return here."

I briefly shifted my focus toward the burnt stump and down to the meadow. Haltingly, I began to speak as I was turning back to Lodehmah, "This is hard to grasp," I said.

As my gaze reached the place where he had been standing, I saw that he was gone! Quickly I looked around but he was nowhere to be seen. On the ground where he had been sitting was a flat rock with two moccasin prints where he had stood when he shouted over the lake; and there was the almost completed circle of little stones. It was then

Harry Owens is a physician involved in international health care, a consultant in international management and stress management, a consultant to St. Charles Medical Center, Oregon, a guest lecturer, a sheep herder, a wilderness survival instructor, a pilot and a horse wrangler.

that I noticed that there were no other footprints leading up to or away from that spot.

I stood there very quietly, almost disbelieving that this meeting had ever taken place. I stared down the meadow for a few minutes trying to collect my thoughts and feelings. Then in the distance I saw the blue heron. It flew slowly and majestically toward me, circled the lake once, and went back down the meadow and out of sight.

I looked down and there in my hand was the solitary little rock. Yes, I said silently to myself, and reached down and placed the rock in the last remaining space; the circle was complete. I cupped my hands around my mouth and shouted out across the lake, "Lo-deh-mah!" Instantly an echo bounced back.

Later that morning I got in my car and started back to Route 66 on my trip home. As I drove, I kept turning the question over in my mind, "What is a healer?" I also wondered what wounds needed healing. But then, Lodehmah said he would help me.

Epilogue: I returned frequently and had other encounters with Lodehmah. Over time and through life experiences, I learned to reach within. In the past two decades, I have visited the area only a few times, mostly out of sentiment. The camp has long since been abandoned, but the meadow and lake are still there. From time to time a blue heron can be seen flying up from the east end of the meadow and circling the lake.

There's no need to give up on life when God's in charge. But if you want to make God laugh, just tell him your plans.

That's Life
(Mary Roush)

That's life, that's what all the people say.
You're riding high in April, shot down in May.

Most of us have sung along with that popular Frank Sinatra tune, but I never realized how prophetic it would prove in my own life.

In the mid-1990s, my husband Skip and I were enjoying post-parenthood. He had taken early retirement from a major corporation a few years before to pursue his entrepreneurial dreams. They were taking shape nicely and he was immensely satisfied seeing his hard work become reality. I was enjoying my career as a psychotherapist with a busy private practice and an active role in the recovery community in my hometown.

We had a lovely home in the city and a mountain retreat with splendid vistas. We traveled widely and celebrated our good fortune to be able to enjoy this time in our lives. We had come through many challenges: raising six children; the demands of corporate life, including relocations; illnesses, deaths and recovery from alcoholism. Life was good.

I've been a puppet, a pauper, a pirate, a poet and a pawn and a king.

I've been up and down and over and out and I know one thing . . .

The day before our 43rd wedding anniversary we were shot down. My husband's entrepreneurial dreams were shattered, blind-sided by betrayal. He not only lost all he had built up, he was also liable for huge losses that pushed us to the brink of bankruptcy.

We were devastated, wounded to the core by the totally unsuspected breach of trust. For weeks we stumbled from day to day like zombies. We tortured ourselves, asking why we hadn't seen it coming. How could we have been so naive?

But I don't let it get me down
'Cause this fine old world it keeps spinning around.

The seasons blurred, one into the next. The losses and legal bills continued to mount. We had to break into our retirement nest egg and had a dramatically reduced income. The future looked bleak indeed.

Becoming One with Our Destiny

Each time I find myself flat on my face,
I pick myself up and get right back in the race.

Today, I know the only way we survived was with the love, concern, support of our family and friends. Our daily prayers and tearful pleas to God were not ignored. We had to learn to truly let go as everything we had worked for was taken away. We had to struggle with hard-won beliefs that something good would come out of so much bad. But we were never alone as we walked it through, one day at a time.

I know that without my 28 years of 12-Step recovery, I would not have been able to build those 24-hour periods into weeks and months. Time and again I would come across books and articles that spoke of forgiveness, or be exposed to others who shared their experiences with it.

For a long time I was too angry to forgive. I found out what "the urge to kill" really means. I struggled to accept that vengeance belongs to the Lord. Fortunately I continued to share my feelings with friends and peers in recovery groups. As I used the program more and more, I identified even more closely with the song.

That's life and as funny as it may seem—
Some people get their kicks stompin' on a dream.

Our losses continued to mount. We decided it was best to sell our home of 21 years and find a way to make our mountain retreat a permanent residence. Later that winter my mother died. Then our daughter and son-in-law moved to Brazil. We had a lot of letting go to do.

Meanwhile I kept seeing clients in my home and Skip readied our mountain home for full-time occupancy. By the fall, we would be ready to move. And I was ready to go. All

Mary Roush is a psychotherapist, mother, grandparent, businesswoman and singer. She has traveled extensively, bringing her experience, strength and hope to people who suffer from alcoholism, especially those in Russia.

the turmoil had taken its toll and I was willing to give up my practice and career as well.

That's life, I tell you I can't deny it.
Many times I thought of quitting, but my heart just ain't gonna buy it.

Ever so slowly, the dim outline of God's plan for us became clear. The stress of corporate life had taken its toll on Skip, who had been diagnosed with diabetes just two years before disaster struck. I had wondered how I would fare if something had happened to him and I had been forced to wrap up his affairs. He had always kept good records and had a trusted attorney who could have helped me through it.

After 18 months of struggle, things became simple again at last. Skip's health improved, we said good-bye to our house and headed to the mountains. The wise investment of assets we managed to salvage has given us a regular source of income and we are nearly debt-free. After selling the house we were able to take a holiday in the sun, free from the dark clouds of fear and doubt. We laughed a lot more and even learned to golf. The irony is that we probably wouldn't have done any of this without God's intervention. We had been far too busy.

We don't call it retirement. Our name for it is Review, Renew, Revitalize. We have time to consider new options and are confident our future will be under God's direction. This is where we and the song part company.

But if there's nothin' changin' come this here July,
I'm gonna roll myself up in a big ball . . . and die.
My, my.

That's life for some people, but not for us.

Life is so simple and uncomplicated when we are in sync with the universe. We are the ones who make it complicated. Going within and learning to follow your own truth gets us back in rhythm with all creation.

Death and Rebirth of a Soul
(Anne Schmitt)

I can hardly remember who I was. It feels like a person that I don't know. I feel sadness when I think of the way that

I was living, or rather existing, as I tried to live up to others' expectations. I had no sense of self; I had surrendered my power to many people and allowed them to destroy me.

I am the oldest of five children from an alcoholic family that lived in a basement apartment. I had many roles as a child: babysitter, family comedian, rescuer, scapegoat and hero. I was angry most of the time and lived in fear, but didn't know it at the time. I did know that I didn't feel good enough.

I had quite a few friends, but I always felt like I was on the outside looking in. In my teen years, I unwittingly set up a pattern of relationship addiction. After I moved to the "big city" at age 18, I found myself in many destructive relationships involving alcoholism and sexual addiction.

When I met my husband he looked different. He was quiet, seemed secure, looked good and came from a "normal" family. The most important part was that this seemingly well-adjusted man wanted this flawed woman. In the early years we had good times; we partied, drank and enjoyed each other sexually.

I wanted a baby, but had medical problems that prevented pregnancy. After surgery, I became pregnant with our first daughter. When she was three months old, I was pregnant again—this time with a son. We looked like the perfect all-American family. Two kids, a home, a dog. But it never filled this large black hole inside which grew day by day like a cancer.

My husband and I were growing apart; I felt restless, trapped. I didn't know what to do or where to go. My husband was drinking and his activities and hobbies kept him from interacting with us. At times I hated him. I joined volunteer groups and finally went to work selling real estate. I needed more outside interests and friends to make my life bearable. I also drank, trying to feel better.

Becoming One with Our Destiny   61

We had been married 22 years when I told him I wanted out. I had the need to control every decision. I said we would stay together until our daughter graduated from high school, which was seven months away. I controlled when the house would go up for sale. I needed to control all of the external events because I was totally out of control inside. I was taking a step that was totally against all of my dreams and values.

Everything was going as well as possible under those trying circumstances: The house was sold, my daughter graduated and I was looking for a condo to buy. My daughter would live with me and my son would live with his dad. We still looked like the perfect family to the outside world.

The house was closing in October and then we would all go on with our lives. And then everything fell apart.

In September I discovered that my husband was seeing another woman he had met in July. Although there should not have been a problem since we were so far in the separation process, his affair pushed me over the edge. All the control I had exhibited had been a sham. The lid came flying off and all the feelings and emotions blew sky high.

I felt suicidal, and totally disconnected from things and people. I wanted back in the relationship, yet I felt powerless and terrified to make it happen. I was in deep emotional pain and thought that being back with him would be a fix. He was my drug.

Instant help was mandatory. I put the divorce on hold and went to treatment, weekly therapy and women's support groups. I lost 25 pounds from the stress.

The house closed. My daughter and I moved into an apartment, my son went to live with friends. I chose not to see my husband or talk to him. I had to stay focused on me since I was having anxiety and panic attacks. The following June, I activated the divorce again, feeling that I would be

Anne Schmitt is a specialist working with those suffering with the HIV virus in Phoenix, Arizona. She loves her role as mother and continues to nurture special friendships. Her eyes light up when she shares the love she has for her work with families who face the pain of living with AIDS.

able to follow through with my support system and a renewed sense of self.

In October I moved to Phoenix, Arizona where the rest of my family lived. My daughter moved with me and my son stayed in Minnesota with his friends. It was painful to leave him but I knew that he needed a chance to survive, too.

Soon after arriving I got my real estate license but hated it. So I returned to college. It was not an easy decision; I was frightened.

I received my certificate in chemical dependency, did my internship at Phoenix Shanti (an agency for people that are infected with the HIV virus) and am now the family counselor there working with the families and friends of HIV-infected persons.

For the first time in my life, I know me. I know my fears, my needs, my old belief system, my destructive patterns. It is not always easy to act on them, but the awareness is there. I have an inner peace that I never knew was possible. I am comfortable being with myself, something that was foreign to me before.

I know now that I am finally on my path—at the right place at the right time. I have worked very hard at my recovery and the rewards are awesome. My life is very full. The one area that I have shied away from are relationships. I needed to build a relationship with myself first so I had something to give to a new love.

When the time is right I know that this will be a reality for me. I fall off the path sometimes, but I know that every time that happens a lesson needs to be learned.

Sometimes, recovery cannot be explained or accounted for. Certain patients embrace love, faith, life, forgiveness and hope in a way that helps them overcome odds, tests and statistics. There seems to be a path to healing and change available for the taking.

The Physiology of Love, Joy & Optimism (Dr. Bernie Siegel)

I am interested in how people embrace life, not how they avoid death.

In January of 1983, John Florio, a 78-year-old landscape gardener, was contemplating retirement. He developed abdominal pain and underwent a GI series, which showed an ulcer. He was treated for one month and re-x-rayed to see if the ulcer had healed. This time, however, it was larger and looked malignant. A biopsy revealed cancer of the stomach.

I first met John in late February when he was referred to my office for surgery. I suggested to him that we get him into the hospital right away since I was going on vacation, and I thought that with a rapidly advancing cancer he ought to have surgery immediately.

He looked at me and said, "You forgot something."

"What did I forget?" I asked.

"It's springtime," he said. "I'm a landscape gardener and I want to make the world beautiful. That way if I survive, it's a gift. If I don't, I will have left a beautiful world."

Two weeks after my vacation, he returned to the office, saying, "The world is beautiful, I'm ready." He looked incredibly well the night after his surgery, with no pain or discomfort. The pathology report revealed he still had a lot of cancer left in him after the operation. I explained that he ought to consider chemotherapy and X-ray therapy to deal with the residual cancer.

"You forgot something," he said.

"What did I forget this time?"

"It's still spring. I don't have time for all that." He was totally at peace, healed rapidly and was out of the hospital well ahead of schedule. His granddaughter, an oncology nurse at Yale, was fully aware of the findings and his choice.

Two weeks later he was back in my office, complaining that his stomach was upset, and I thought, "Aha, it's the cancer again." It turned out to be a virus, which I treated.

Becoming One with Our Destiny

In March of 1987, I arrived at my office and saw John's name in the chart rack.

"You must have the wrong chart," I said to the nurse.

"No, that's the right chart," she said.

"Then there must be two people with the same name."

"No, no," she insisted, "he's sitting in there."

I showed her his pathology report to explain why I assumed she had made a mistake. If you think pathology reports predict the future for an individual, it wouldn't seem possible that I could be seeing John four years after his operation. But that's who I saw when I walked into my examining room.

I feared that his visit would be related to cancer. Before I could ask him anything, he said, "Don't forget, this is only my second postoperative visit." I think he wanted to make sure the insurance would cover it.

"But why are you here?" I asked.

"I'd like to know what you can eat after a stomach operation."

"After four years, anything!" I said laughing. "But, seriously, why are you here?"

"I have a hernia from lifting boulders."

Since he refused to be admitted to the hospital, I repaired it under local anesthesia on an outpatient basis, and he was off and running again. If he rested at all I'd be surprised, even though he promised to have two young men do his normal work for the first few weeks after surgery.

John is one of those exceptional patients who defy understanding. I have learned that all of these exceptional patients have stories to tell and lessons to teach. It's not just a matter of being lucky or having "well-behaved" diseases (slow-growing tumors, "spontaneous" remissions and so forth).

Bernie Siegel, M.D., is the author of How to Live Between Office Visits and Love, Medicine & Miracles. *He has brought hope to families suffering from cancer.*

There is a biology of the individual as well as a biology of the disease, each affecting the other.

It's now six years after surgery and John celebrated his 83rd birthday. What happened to his cancer?

I don't know if his immune system eliminated it or if it's still in there, enjoying John's life so much that it's going along for the ride. John's ability to live and love and his passion about his life's work are therapeutic.

He sent an article about himself in the local newspaper. He is quoted: "If I find a little marigold just lying there, I feel so sorry for it I just put a hole in the ground with my finger and plant it." The article ends by saying

"Today . . . John is still on the job, planting and pruning. He loves it. And like the legendary cowboy who proudly professes he wants to die in the saddle with his boots on, he says when his turn comes 'I always pray that I'll die at work, gardening.'"

Working outdoors, John maintains what I call a celestial connection, and, like the patients in the hospital who have been shown to heal faster when their room has a view of the sky, he is healthier because of it. John is too busy living to be sick. That's his real secret. But how, in scientific terms, do we account for him? What can we learn from him? Is there really a physiology of optimism, peace, love and joy? I like to think there is.*

We never really know what we're made of until confronted with a challenge that tests us to the limit. Then we have the opportunity to discover not only who we are, but also what matters most to us.

A Second Chance
(Nancy Waits)

As fall 1993 approached, I thought that my life couldn't be better. I married a man I had known for 20 years and was finding each day a new joy. We had both endured painful marriages and found our new life together was beautiful and rewarding. Sharing feelings, finding peace through prayer,

---

*Pages 9-11 from PEACE, LOVE AND HEALING by BERNIE SIEGEL, M.D. Copyright ©1989 by Bernie S. Siegel, M.D.
Reprinted by permission of HarperCollins Publishers, Inc.

meditation, humor, we learned what not to do, and how to schedule quality time together. Life was good.

On a beautiful October day, I was leaving work when I remembered my annual mammogram appointment. My first thought was to reschedule, but an inner voice told me to keep it. I became concerned when the technician took many more views of my left breast than in previous years. I was asked to see my surgeon immediately.

After he had studied the X ray and examined my breast, my doctor scheduled a biopsy. When he told me, "You have breast cancer," I looked around to see to whom he was speaking.

After the initial shock, I had to make many decisions quickly. With full knowledge of my choices, these decisions were made methodically, with no second thoughts. I knew I wanted the cancer removed from my body as completely and promptly as possible. I also wanted immediate reconstruction utilizing my own body tissue. This choice allowed me to go into surgery with a more positive thought: "I'll go to sleep with my old breast and wake up with a new one."

The next hurdle was chemotherapy. I had decided to have the six-month course of treatment recommended by my oncologist as insurance to kill any errant cancer cells. I felt that I could get through anything as long as I knew that there was a beginning and an ending to it. However, the initial shock of having cancer stayed with me for some time.

After the first sessions of chemotherapy, I knew what to expect. I started to think of the drugs as little "Pac Men" eating up all the bad cancer cells and fighting to rid my system of them. Since my energy level after the treatments was low, there were many hours to think and ponder the rest of my life.

My friends and family became my support system. At this stage of my life, my friends are those with whom I have traveled life's path for some time. This was one more step on that journey, with no pretenses allowed.

I found it hard to believe that I had cancer since there was no history of it in our family. I told myself, "I'm a nurse, married to a surgeon. We take care of other people; I'm not a sick person." My next thoughts were that I was too young to have this malignancy.

When illness struck my priorities quickly changed. What was really important to me? My family, my loving husband of three years, my parents, my five brothers and sisters, my nieces and nephews, my "inherited" children and my grandchildren, became my intense focus points. All of us shared what we meant to one another and planned our times together to reflect our support and love.

Reading has become a spiritual time for me. My daily meditations that my husband and I shared took on a new and more relevant meaning. Their lessons are ones that I am now living. Dr. Bernie Siegel's books, *Love, Medicine & Miracles* and *Peace, Love & Healing*, were particularly strengthening for me.

These days I am better able to listen to the songs of the birds and rejoice in them. This special time has given me a greater appreciation of everyday spirituality: the beauty of sunshine, the moonlight on the lake at night, the deep blue sky against the pine trees and seeing God's face in the cloud formations. How many of us get this second chance to really be a part of our surroundings and enjoy this beauty?

Humor is also an integral part of our daily lives. My husband and I now work together in his office where we have found laughter to be the best medicine. I think not taking yourself too seriously helps us find that special spark in other people. Since a large part of my husband's practice includes breast cancer patients, I have found opportunities

Nancy Waits, wife, mother and grandmother, is a general surgical nursing manager and educator at Northside Hospital in Atlanta. She and her husband enjoy spending time at their mountain cabin in North Carolina, playing golf and traveling.

to share my experience with them. I try to impart strength and hope for their recovery.

Pets are particularly comforting also. Our two cats, Maggie and Meow, can feel the positive energy between my husband and I, and have been able to share in our love. One particular day when I was feeling low from the chemotherapy, our cat Meow seemed to know he was there to help me. Every time I went back and forth to the bathroom, he was right there with me; his purring finally calmed me and I was able to relax and let the nausea pass. He knew I needed him that afternoon.

I thought naps during the day were only for young children and aging adults. I have now learned to welcome an afternoon nap; I can feel the healing in my spirit from the quick rest. I'm now energized enough to take my two-mile walk near the river where I marvel at the difference in my life yet again. I feel as if I have indeed been give a second chance to appreciate all the things God has given me!

I am truly grateful to God for all these gifts which surround me everyday. I know my Higher Power is guiding and guarding me on my journey.

Moving from sick to well, from wounded to healed, occurs organically in imperceptible increments. The ability to appreciate the subtlety of the process is a sign of wisdom, depth and presence. While change can be dramatic, it is often the breath of air wafting lightly across one's cheek that signals real change.

I Wanted a Relationship
(John Friel)

The year was 1980. I had been single for five years following a painful divorce. I had tried dating a number of different women but none of these early relationships seemed to go anywhere. I was lonely, confused and desperate. Then one day I made a commitment to stop looking for a marital partner for at least a year to clear my soul.

It was a difficult time, raising my children, struggling with career crises and my alcoholism. I helped a lot of people with projects, developed new interests and honored my

John C. Friel, Ph.D. and Linda D. Friel, M.A., are licensed psychologists in private practice in St. Paul, Minnesota, and authors of the best-selling Adult Children: The Secrets of Dysfunctional Families, An Adult Child's Guide to What's "Normal," The Grown-Up Man, Rescuing Your Spirit *and* The Soul Of Adulthood: Opening the Doors.

commitment. During that frigid Minnesota winter, I would fantasize in my journal that I lived back in my native Northern California, or on the Big Island of Hawaii, where the tropical sea breeze would take the lonely chill from my heart forever.

I hated it, endured it, fought with it and prayed for patience and direction. I tried to medicate myself, fought with that, endured some more, tried harder and waited some more. I was action-oriented and controlling and sorely lacked patience. The waiting, day in and day out, brought the most significant spiritual deepening for me.

The "transforming incident" occurred about 10 months into this process, but it was the loneliness and the waiting and healing of old wounds that constituted the actual transformation.

One evening as I sat at my journal, discouraged and yet feeling that I had no right to complain because I hadn't grown up enough yet, I wrote: "I wish that just one bit of warmth or graciousness would come into my life."

The next day as I approached the indoor swimming pool on the nearby college campus, towel in hand, I made eye contact with a woman I had met very briefly several years before. An electricity passed between the two of us that was so sudden, so startling, so unexpected, so exciting and so wonderful.

Without further ado Linda and I fell in love. It was a moment of magic and grace, all because of those cold, lonely winter nights; the boring, empty afternoons; and the desperately painful holidays during which I struggled, waited, and hoped, that made it possible.

PART THREE

TRANSFORMATION: BECOMING MORE OF WHO WE ARE

The Body, Mind and Spirit

*M*an *demonstrates in his own*
nature a pressure toward fuller and fuller
Being, more and more perfect actualization of his
own humanness in exactly the same naturalistic,
scientific sense that an acorn may be said to be
"pressing toward" being an oak tree.

—Abraham Maslow

hen we dance with our bodies, something happens to how we feel inside and how we look to others: The heartbeat quickens, the focus on our muscles and limbs grows sharper and we feel our physical presence more acutely in time and space. On the outside, we look as though we have come to life and are charged with expressive energy that can range from a smoldering tango or poignant pas-de-deux to an exuberant polka or smooth-moving samba. In short, we are transformed.

When we dance with the Spirit, we are also transformed. We feel different inside—more alive, more connected to our true self, to others and to God (or whatever we perceive as our Higher Power). We also appear different to others. They see someone fully engaged with the world, but not overwhelmed by it; someone who deliberately chooses how to express himself or herself.

To transform, whether in body or spirit, means to change in appearance and nature without altering our meaning or value. This definition implies that at all stages of being we are meaningful and valuable. To enter a transformation process means to add to, enhance and embellish what already exists. It does not mean going from something less desirable to something more desirable. It is important to know our value at all times so that when transformation occurs you become more of who you are, you do not become someone else. An acorn does not become a chicken, it becomes a tree.

Often, however, there are moments in life where we either feel pulled or drawn to a new life experience. Sometimes things happen to us that we were not expecting: an illness, accident or loss that takes us to a new life experience. Whether or not the change is of our choosing, it may hold the potential to be an enlightening event.

Frequently, transformation comes out of "stuck" spots. There are those times when we know some part of life is not working. We know it's time for a change—that we can't stay the same or go backwards, yet we don't know

The Body, Mind and Spirit 79

how to go forward. If we are willing to be open and alert for clues, change does take place.

Many people are curious and willing to explore new paths if the time is right. Transformation is not a one-time event; it happens over time and takes many directions. It occurs through interactions with other people and with our environment, through the work we do and the ways we have fun and nurture our spirit. It happens as we make choices and decisions triggered by events around us and within us.

Often change starts with a restlessness, a void or an emptiness. When we are in that state, we have an opportunity to discover who we are and where we came from and to select a new direction for the future. In the emptiness we may experience an unexpected flash of understanding that enables us to recognize our connection to God, a Higher Power, a divine presence.

These times of emptiness are periods of transformation. Anthony Padavano defines this dynamic of transformation in *Belief in Human Life*.

There is a great deal of difference between loss, change, and transformation. A loss is a step backward; a change is an opportunity; transformation is a step forward. The common denominator in these three realities is the fact that one must give up something. It is possible for both loss and change to lead to transformation, but it is not possible for transformation to occur unless something is lost and something is changed.

The Sign
(Marty's Story)

After my divorce I was depressed and found it very hard to cope as a single parent. I was terrified that I wouldn't be able to provide for my children and the bank would repossess our home. One night I fell into troubled sleep after deciding I really needed to participate in more extensive therapy.

Prior to that night, I had been angry with God more than once for not being available. I had probably even dared God to show me some sign that he cared. I awakened soon after falling into a restless sleep. Since I was in the habit of recording my dreams, I reached for the paper and pencil on my nightstand, hoping I'd be able to decipher my handwriting in the morning. Just then I heard a rushing or whirring sound, like the wind. I sat up to stare at a spinning cocoon of the brightest, whitest light swirling into my bedroom. It continued to spin upright just inside my doorway.

A clear resonant voice said only two words that sounded both near and far: "Live" and "Believe." Then darkness descended once again.

The next morning I read on the note pad "spinning cocoon" and the two spoken words. A few days later while sharing this dream vision at the therapy workshop, I began to question whether this had been a dream. It had certainly seemed real. As I heard myself start questioning myself, I realized that out of a real despair had come this unmistakably clear sign. I had heard the voice of God—it was a miracle. I never again questioned whether my life mattered, but instead began to pray for strength and courage to maintain the commitment to my recovery.

Al-Anon's Message
(From Ray)

I attend Al-Anon* meetings regularly. They have transformed my life. I never leave a meeting without feeling energized. As others share their experience, strength and hope, I am touched by a room full of people lifting my spirit in the process.

I'm sure other 12-Step meetings have the same power with the people who attend.

---

* Author's note: Alcoholics Anonymous, the original 12-Step group, now has more than 1,790,000 members in 89,000 groups in 120 countries. Each person in each group is an angel to the other members. AA's influence extends far beyond its membership. It has also been said that the methods and beliefs of Alcoholics Anonymous represent America's single most significant contribution to the world's rich stock of unique traditions of spiritual development.

The Patterns of Transformation

Life is a daring adventure or it's nothing at all.

—Helen Keller

While each transformation is unique, there is a pattern that most changes follow which we can easily learn to recognize as we go through the process.

1. Become aware that there's got to be a better way—identify the issue.
2. Build a base of spiritual, mental, physical health—take care of each part of the self on a daily basis.
3. Face feelings—talk about it, face hurt, fear, anger, guilt, etc.

4. Start healing by looking at what you are running from—confront and examine the issue and behaviors around it.
5. Undergo a rebirth and discover personal power—resolve the issue and begin changing behavior.
6. Face relationships and clear up pain between people—take the necessary action to make amends.
7. Serve others and leave the world a better place—find a way to contribute to the universe.

Bureaucracy
(Patrick's Story)

When my Canadian-born wife Angela and I had decided to move from West Palm Beach, Florida, to Vancouver, British Columbia, we really didn't know what was in store for us.

We had moved to Florida four years before from Montreal, where I had become a landed-immigrant, the equivalent of a permanent resident in the U.S. I wasn't supposed to have been away from Canada that long, so I called the Canadian immigration authorities in Ottawa and asked what I should do.

"Just come back and present yourself at the border," they said. It sounded too easy.

After selling our house and quitting our jobs, we loaded up the truck with our two-year-old son and our four cats. We drove across America and presented ourselves at the border, fully expecting that I would be readmitted without incident, despite the overlong, unreported absence.

"Oh no," said the immigration official, "there's no way you can just come back like that. You'll have to reapply. It could take months."

Crestfallen and with no back-up plan, I told them what the Ottawa immigration officials had said. They made phone calls to hash out the situation. An hour later we were told we had permission to return. The person in charge shook his head.

"None of us has ever heard of this kind of thing happening," he said.

This angelic intervention had unforeseen benefits. In the first two years after our arrival in Vancouver, where Angela's mother lived, they were able work through many of the unresolved issues between them. When Angela's mother suddenly passed away, my wife was thankful for the good fortune of returning in time to resolve these issues before her mother died. The prospect of starting new lives, with no jobs or support networks, also led us both into recovery programs.

A Safe Place
(From Elizabeth)

During my last two years of high school, I had many difficulties at home and with my classmates. I had a teacher who gave me a place where I could be safe and quiet, even though she didn't know all the details of my troubles. She let me stay in her office during study hall and grade papers. I was always grateful for her understanding but it took 10 years after my graduation for me to finally thank her for the unconditional acceptance of my situation and her offering me a safe haven when I needed it most.

TRANSFORMING PEOPLE

---

*We and God have business with
each other through the spirit, and in opening
ourselves to God and each other, our
deepest destiny is fulfilled.*

—William James

People open to transforming themselves lead lives of opportunity, awareness and freedom. Those who maintain the status quo exist in monotonous conformity, stuck, stunted and fearful of change. In the chart below, I have contrasted some salient characteristics of people willing to change with those who are not.

Transforming People	Status Quo Maintainers
Resist conformity	Conform to others
Invent new lifestyles	Act like victims
Have creative personalities	Are followers
Define own goals	Have poorly defined goals
Are directed by inner selves	Are other-directed
Belive personal experiences	Believe what others believe
Live in the present	Live in the past or future
Accept pain as necessary	Hide from pain
Become whole	Remain fragmented
Have solid value systems	Have contradictory values
Are direct and simple	Are confused and complicated
Are decisive	Are indecisive
Feel free	Feel stuck and powerless

Relationships and Transformation

When a person is singing and cannot lift his voice, and another one comes and sings along, the first will be able to lift his voice. That is the secret of the bond between spirits.

—from Jewish writings

---

ot surprisingly, transforming people and maintainers of the status quo have very different relationships. We see the differences in our relationships with ourselves, our friends and mates, and especially with our Higher Power.

Transforming People	Status Quo Maintainers
Liberating and freeing	Manipulative and controlling
Honest	Deceptive
Risking	Safe and conforming
Initiators and co-creators	Joiners and followers
Independent love	Mutual dependence
Original	Conventional
Accept love as a relationship we create	Believe we "fall" in love
Find commitment exciting and fulfilling	Find commitment restricting
Shared spirituality	Embarrassed by spirituality

As you can see, spirituality plays a large role in transforming a person's life. French philosopher and theologian, Teilhard de Chardin, wrote about the active life of the transformer.

The longer I live, the more I feel that true repose consists in "renouncing" one's own self, by which I mean making up one's mind to admit that there is no importance whatever in being "happy" or "unhappy" in the usual meaning of the words. Personal success or personal satisfaction are not worth another thought if one does achieve them, not worth worrying about if they evade one or are slow in coming. All that is really worthwhile is action—faithful action, for the world, and in God. Before one can see that and live by it, there is a sort of threshold to cross, or a reversal to be made in what appears to be man's general habit of thought, but once that gesture has been made, that freedom is yours, freedom to work and love.

Transformation is not something that takes place outside the sphere of everyday life. To see how it works in our day-to-day doing and thinking, it may help to take a new look at old spiritual terms: chaos, commitment and redemption.

Chaos: Life is inherently uncertain, uncontrollable and unpredictable. We feel its chaotic energy in the struggles of family life, work and relationships— lonely and tension-filled days and fretful nights that never seem to end. These forms of disorder are wasted time and energy unless they can be seen as opportunities to find a higher understanding of our spirituality and the presence of the divine.

Commitment: As each of us tries to grope our way through the dark and gloomy night, we can commit ourselves to the meanings we find in each situation. We can make choices to illuminate our human condition.

Redemption: As we discover the meaning of our lives by making choices, we have an opportunity to help create change with the universe. We can become partners in day-to-day miracle-making.

With these concepts in mind, we can see now that if we go through life denying ourselves the pain of awareness and risk, we also deny the possibility of connecting with our spirit in personal redemption. If we continue to avoid our feelings of anger, rage, fear and hurt, we consign ourselves to a safe life of triviality and boredom.

Comfort in Verse
(From Patrick)

A friend was dying. Although we weren't close, I knew him well enough to take a turn at the bedside vigil as his life slipped slowly away. I sat listening to his labored breathing as he slept and gazed upon his ravaged body. A poem came to me, one that celebrated the joy he had brought to so many in his short lifetime. I gave the poem to his parents, hoping it might somehow ease the heartbreak. Months later I received a letter saying how the poem had become a treasure for them, a source of solace that they shared with friends and family through the waves of grief that followed the loss of their son.

An Angel in Adversity
(Julie's Story)

Several years ago my mother, father and I were in a serious car accident. The weather was very unsettled that day and we had decided that my father would drive his large car and we would leave my smaller vehicle at home. We felt the heavier vehicle would be safer under the adverse weather conditions. This turned out to be a good choice.

About 11 miles into our trip home, we were hit head-on by a car driving down the wrong side of the road. All three of us were sitting in the front seat. The first thing I remember was glass shattering and a hissing sound. Then there was complete silence.

"Mom . . . Dad, are you okay?" I asked. There was no response. Then my father said, "Yes, get out, I smell fire."

I was able to move, but Dad's leg was stuck under the gas pedal. Working around my mother, who lay inert, I was able to free my father and get him out of the car.

I tugged at my mother and soon we were all standing outside of the car. I looked in the other vehicle and was overcome by the strong smell of alcohol; there was no body. Finally, a car came by, which I later learned almost hit me and swerved into the ditch instead. The driver offered to take me to get help.

After a couple of days in the hospital I learned that my mother, who had been up and walking immediately after the accident, had 22 broken bones, a crushed foot, two broken legs and several other serious injuries. My father had facial injuries and had been walking around on a broken leg. I also learned that the other individual was our neighbor's son who was intoxicated. He died as a result of the accident.

I believe that someone looked over us that day. This tragic incident also opened a door to recovery for my family. It brought my father and I closer and opened our eyes to alcohol's destructiveness. This awareness and the family closeness stays with me today. It's a shame that it takes tragedy to find love and understanding between a father and daughter. But I wouldn't trade it for the world.

Seeking Balance High and Low

---

*God does not die on the day we cease
to believe in a personal God, but we die on the day
our lives cease to be enlightened by the wondering
about the source of all creation.*

—Dag Hammarskjöld

One of the important lessons I have learned over time is the value of balance in transformations. They can be unsettling experiences for us and those close to us. We get so excited about our new smorgasbord of possibilities and options that we become gluttons in our eagerness to sample what life has to offer. Famished, we are tempted by the feast. We lose sight of the path we have traveled and we become imbalanced in our recovery.

96   *Transformation: Becoming More of Who We Are*

When we have a sense of proportion, poise and equilibrium in activities, we don't become spiritual groupies or transformation junkies. A thread of harmony runs through our lives and we keep in focus the knowledge that there are different levels of consciousness in spiritual growth. Many masters, spiritual teachers, mystics and sages have commented on the varieties of spiritual growth and levels of spiritual consciousness. They are all part of a natural unfolding, each a necessary part of the whole.

1. *Survival,* the most basic awareness of being, is characterized by the drive for self-preservation. Some suffer at this fundamental level as they self-destruct with sex, alcohol, drugs, food, smoking, gambling or other addictive behaviors.

2. *Emotional Awakening* comes from being able to feel. Suffering can involve repressing feelings of painful experiences, bottling up feelings and energy.

3. *Intellect* is concerned with producing thoughts and ideas, as well as the ability to analyze and understand. Professionals often suffer at this level because they have been trained to believe that science and knowledge are the only kinds of truth that count.

4. *Acceptance* comes when we develop the ability to forgive ourselves and others. Some people have difficulty because they do not want to give up resentments and remain fixed in the past, or they prefer a state of conflict.

5. *Clarity* is the development of natural, inner knowledge. Some people are often afraid to trust their intuitions.

Seeking Balance High and Low 97

6. *Love* is the consciousness of being, even if one's affection is not acknowledged, accepted or returned. Without the gift of faith, one risks feeling as though love alone will make one feel whole or happy. In doing so, one forgets the crucial connections to our co-Creator.

7. *Enlightenment* is a connection to the Higher Power. We feel at home in the universe. The danger comes in forgetting that it takes balance to achieve this level of awareness.

As people undergo transformations and move to different stages of spiritual consciousness, there is a tendency to feel as if they're climbing higher. Spiritual consciousness, however, is not an ordinary ladder. There is no "higher" and "lower" in spiritual consciousness; it encompasses all levels.

The celebrated guru who professes to have reached enlightenment has not moved closer to God-consciousness if all other levels are not in operation. He or she remains unenlightened.

Father Joseph Martin captures the essence of balance with these words: "If I'm in a car accident, for goodness sake, don't take me to group therapy. Take me to a hospital!"

We are mortal as well as spiritual beings, and we have to live in the world. It's part of our job. If God wanted us all to live only in the world of higher consciousness and evolution, he would take us to that place. He wants us to have the experience of fully living with feet on the ground, solidly connected with him, and fully experiencing everything in between.

The Dance
(Mary's Tale)

When I was in eighth grade our school put on an operetta. A group of us were chosen to dance the minuet. I was thrilled to be picked and practiced it to perfection. When the teacher said our costume was a long gown and matching bonnet, I knew there was no way my parents could afford it and I'd have to drop out. It broke my heart.

My dearest friend and neighbor was also in the operetta. Her mother was a wonderful seamstress and had just finished her beautiful gown and bonnet with rows of lace.

Unbeknownst to me, she had told her mom of my dilemma. Her mother went up to her attic and brought down a bunch of old white ruffled curtains, dyed them a pretty pink color and made me a gown and bonnet. They were gorgeous. I felt like a fairy princess and everyone said how pretty I looked as I danced the minuet.

No one knew I had two secret angels that made it happen. Today, my angel friend and I talk and visit each other when we can. Her mother remains my other angel.

MEDITATION

*The Kingdom of God
is within you.*

—Luke 17:21

The gathering of the spiritually awake is growing. I am part of that movement; if I keep striving for something better in my life, there will be no stagnation. Inner power and inner peace are mine for the asking. I will not spend time over past failures. I will count my lessons learned from failures as rungs on the ladder of progress.

Dreaming
(Peter's Story)

When I was five years old, living in New England, I would lie in the grass and look up at the blue sky. These were tough times—my dad was hospitalized with TB and my mother was caring for a newborn baby.

One day a neighbor who worked in a local nursery needed to make a delivery to a private school in the next town and invited my mother and me to drive with him and his wife. He spoke proudly of the preparatory school, its beautiful campus, and its students and their achievements. One student even became president of the United States.

I announced quite proudly that I would one day attend this school. Considering our financial circumstances this seemed like a very remote possibility, but I remember my mother smiling and saying "We will see."

A decade later I had a paper route in the hospital where my father worked. One of the patients, an older gentleman recovering from a lung disease, took an interest in me. He asked about my hopes and dreams. After he talked to my father, he offered me a scholarship to any preparatory school of my choice.

This man had never finished grammar school but founded a successful advertising agency and ran for the U.S. Senate. He believed in education and helping young people like myself. His only stipulation was that I do the same for another young person later in my life.

Fortunately, because of the opportunity this incredibly generous man gave me, I have been able to help others, just as he helped me realize my dreams.

THE MEANING OF LIFE

*M*an will hereafter be called
to account for depriving himself of all good
things the world has to offer.

—The Talmud

We are, of course, free to ignore our spiritual development and decline the invitation to join the dance of destiny. If we choose not to take the opportunity to, we stay stuck and may be faced with an inner emptiness.

This void is a spiritual vacuum that will keep us compulsively searching for fixes or solutions for our inner emptiness. Until we are touched by spiritual awakening and find ourselves filled with a sense of purpose and serenity, a restlessness will haunt us.

Spirituality is a quality that infuses life with meaning, energizing us and providing a rationale for life and death.

Intellect, science and technology can suggest how to use our bodies and our minds effectively and help us with the how of existence. But they offer little help in giving us answers to the whys that we yearn for. Why the rush? Why the pain and turmoil? Why the loneliness and emptiness? Intellect, science and technology remain silent. The answers will be found in the world of the Spirit.

There are many ways to avoid joining the dance. If I just keep busy . . . or have enough to look forward to . . . or follow all the traditions and do everything I should, then my life will be happy and fulfilled. Surely it will have meaning.

Will it? Don't count on it.

I'm reminded of a lady I met a while back who invited me for coffee. Once seated, she told me what a hectic week she had: she had been shopping, spent too much money and was out of sorts with her husband. But she had one more gift to get and then she would be done shopping for Christmas.

"Are you enjoying yourself?" I asked.

She looked surprised. "What does that have to do with anything?"

She added that she felt guilty being away from her children and resentful over the money spent. She wished the holidays were over so she could relax. This poor woman was too caught up in what she felt she should be doing. When I returned home, I felt sad because of her emptiness. I also felt and powerless to help her.

The Meaning of Life   103

In contrast, another friend called me on Thanksgiving Day to wish me happy Thanksgiving. She told me that she and her husband were alone for dinner that day, but what a glorious day it was. Her life brimmed with meaning and purpose; to stay home was a time of real thanksgiving for her. It was a day to take time to be grateful and to appreciate the abundance of happiness. She reflected true inner peace.

Where does this inner peace, this love of life, come from? The great teachers and spiritual masters have taught it and inspired countless people to seek it, but it is something that we must find within. All the sermons and self-sacrifices become meaningless gestures and hollow noise if we do not have love and understanding for ourselves and each other.

How do we get in touch with the Spirit? The best way I know is through prayer and meditation. A time of prayer and meditation allows us to turn off the clatter in our minds so that we can integrate our experience with knowledge and come to a more fundamental understanding of reality. Through prayer and meditation, we get back to basics and accept the reality of life as a gift to be explored. A time of serenity eases the pressure of daily events and allows us to discern our priorities.

We can see that God doesn't want us to DO something, he calls us to BE somebody. We must unfold and fulfill ourselves in all aspects of our being, detecting our specialness and nurturing it.

When we put aside our urge to rigidly control ourselves and others, we can respond to the Spirit and come to know our inner power, accepting it and ceasing our

104   *Transformation: Becoming More of Who We Are*

defensiveness and fear. We can share power with others and not be diminished or impoverished. Love grows, allowing the bond between people to be one of mutual respect and caring. In each of our lives is at least one other person who may never know any other love but the one we share. That sharing of love is part of our mission.

Power comes from within and being attuned to our inner strengths through prayer and meditation allows us to look within instead of outside to discover why we are special. Life no longer perplexes us; we fit as snugly as a piece in a jigsaw puzzle.

As we come to know and accept ourselves, our inner Spirit is released. Prayer and meditation are not reserved for ministers, saints and mystics. Spirit is inherent in each of us, awaiting discovery, like kindling awaiting the spark of awareness that will burst into a holy flame.

We are energy cells, empowered to co-create, to work with a Creator to make meaning in a world that needs change and redemption. Our progress and direction come from a power within ourselves, and we can call that power God.

Faith Goes with the Flow

od lets us experience complete and total helplessness from time to time in order to remind us that as mortals we are powerless. But, at the same time, as persons using our emotional, physical and spiritual strengths, we *are* powerful. Freedom comes in accepting the reality of life and the reality of not controlling ourselves or others. Faith comes in trusting the Spirit when our defenses crumble so our strength will prevail.

Searchers miss this mystery of faith and meaning because they cannot grasp it. The irony is that we can only be grasped by it. Faith is not an intellectual concept, something to understand, debate and collect data on. Faith is an attitude, a readiness, a willingness to accept unquestioningly. We sense it, feel it and know it in ourselves and in others.

We feel faith when we are with someone we love; when we are aware of life's awesome mystery; when we experience the thrill of rebirth; and when we get to the point of accepting ourselves.

Faith is the thread we hang on to when our life is falling apart. We experience it when we see the power of an ocean and the fragility of a dried-up dandelion. Faith is the warmth we feel when another person understands and accepts us with open arms. At such times we are in touch with the Spirit.

In describing this gift of faith, I am not saying that we always feel vibrant and confident. Even the most spiritual and most faithful among us have dark moments and gloomy moods. But with faith we have resilience, a reservoir of courage, strength and hope to draw on when we encounter pain. And we stand ready to be used by the Spirit in whatever plan God has for our lives.

When we feel the Spirit, it's like coming out of a fog. We know it can get foggy again, but we also know that there's sunshine above and the Spirit will shine through once again. The light of the Spirit frees people, unburdens them, fosters growth and transformation.

We are part of the plan of the universe, but when we resist our spiritual side, we falter and become tense and restless and feel trapped in a spiritual void.

The Spirit comes to us like wind blowing through our lives, taking away pretense, games, phoniness. The Spirit leaves us raw, exposed, vulnerable and real. We are who we are. We are free to figure out the meaning of life and to help set others free.

As spirituality seekers, we have two tasks of the Spirit: The first is to carve out our own singular meaning in life through growth and self-awareness. The second task is to open ourselves to the mystery of our place in redemption and understand how pain can be turned into inner peace.

Dag Hammarskjöld wrote: "The longest journey is the journey inward, for he who has chosen his destiny has started upon his quest for the source of his being." The journey is not grounded in belief. It is grounded in faith. Believers have a preconceived idea of how things should be. Those with faith know that life is rich and full of surprises. Believers cling to creeds and officially sanctioned truth. Those with faith are guided by a deep and abiding trust in a Higher Power and in their own inner strength. Faith is a letting go and an acceptance of the life of the Spirit—a flowing with reality.

The life of the Spirit can be scary, for it involves venturing into unaccustomed realms. It is learning a new dance complete with missteps, being out of sync, even falling down. Naturally we feel tentative at first, but in time we adjust. It is not easy to admit that our egos are limited and there is a wider existence that can affect us. It's hard to drop our defenses and expose ourselves and take risks, trusting to faith in the face of the unknown.

And it's difficult to admit how much we need one another. It is much easier and less risky to cling to familiar patterns and old conventional answers, even though new life is struggling to burst forth. The spirit of reality is already here, and so is new life.

Swan Lake
(Mary Jo's Story)

In the middle of an afternoon I noticed a flurry of activity a short distance from the shore in the lake in front of my home. A small rowboat had one person in it and six people swimming in circles and taking turns diving. My initial thought was to ask, "Why would anyone be doing synchronized swimming here?"

Quickly I realized that all was not right. A 28-year-old man had been scuba diving and the person in the boat was his wife. The diver, Joe, had surfaced after several dives and told his wife, Sue, that he was having trouble breathing and as she watched helplessly, he put his hands up into the air and went down.

Sue cried out for help and four young people in a nearby boat, three of them trained lifeguards, went to her assistance. Those three, plus two young kids who had been working at a neighbor's house, were the heads I saw in the water. After several futile attempts to find Joe, they just remained in the water to mark the spot where Sue had last seen her husband.

Within minutes, our front yard was filled with emergency medical vehicles, deputies, EMTs, divers, firemen and equipment handlers. A deputy brought the young wife to our pier and we took her into our home to escape the eyes of the spectators and news media who were gathering on the banks.

Sue was with us for five hours before the searchers recovered her husband's body. During that time my husband and I, along with a good friend and neighbor, sat with Sue. She called her father to come and wait with her.

But the hardest call she had to make was to Joe's parents to tell them their son was missing.

Faith Goes with the Flow

We sat together, cried, prayed and listened to her stories about her dear Joe. They had been married a year and a half and he was her best friend. They had moved only a few months earlier into a new home and had just finished the landscaping. They took the day off from work to be together and have some fun. Joe was happy to be diving again. As we sat and cried and prayed, we felt pure love for this strong young woman and her Joe.

I saw many angels that day. The swimmers who dove for Joe, the deputy who patiently took information from Sue, the divers who methodically searched the lake bottom, the EMTs who stood by hoping to be needed, the support group who brought food for the rescue workers, the fire department chaplain who gave comfort, and my neighbors who offered the use of their boats, anchors and ropes to aid the searchers and never complained about the heavy trucks on their beautiful lawns.

One particular neighbor spent hours on the water driving his boat for the divers and several days later took Joe's family and Sue out onto the water again so they could leave flowers.

As the ordeal neared an end, the boaters maneuvered their vessels to block the television cameras from taping Joe's body being lifted from his watery grave. Then the support personnel stood shoulder to shoulder on the pier and shoreline, not just to block the cameras, but also in silent respect for a man they never knew. There were more than a hundred angels at the lake that day.

The fire chief and county sheriff later sent letters to say thank you and the EMT called a few days later to ask how we are doing. Sue's father sent us flowers in the midst of his own sorrow. And Sue wrote, saying we are often in her thoughts and signed her letter, "All my love . . . I will never forget you."

Lastly, a very special angel sent a message to us the morning after Joe's death. A beautiful swan flew over the lake and landed in the spot where he went down. We had not seen a swan on our lake for years nor have we seen one since. It quietly swam in a circle a few times and then flew off leaving behind a feeling of peace and serenity.

A GOOD TIME
TO GROW

People in change remind me of springtime. In fact, I sometimes refer to them as Springtime People since they radiate new life, new hope and new warmth.

Springtime People embody God's plan and purpose that each of us should be free to become fully ourselves. When the sun shines on a garden, the flowers open to reveal marvels of intricate color and design. So, too, with a transforming person as he or she unfolds in the glow of the Spirit.

No more inner emptiness and aimlessness. No more spiritual void. From a transforming heart comes a unique melody, a song of harmony and self-containment welling up and flowing from inner tranquility. They are the ones who move in harmony with the music of life and literally spring forward in the dance with destiny.

If people were like music, we could see that it takes a clear and specific note to produce a good sound and when several notes come together, we have music. Becoming a whole person is one element to the harmony that is produced when others join. This is the chorus of Spirit we flow with as co-Creators in transformation. And with each transformation, we build a little more heaven on earth.

We know we are becoming transformed when we accept that:

1. We have all the resources we need. We are enough just the way we are.
2. We create our reality based on what we think and how we feel, not on how others think and feel about us.
3. We all have power of choice.
4. The universe is cooperative.

After transformation we can easily choose and accept what happens in life, because we know that God is a part of what is happening. When we can accept some divine order, we can learn to let go and work with the universe, allowing God to support us.

A Short Visit from a Small Angel
(Joan's Tale)

The angels in our lives come in many shapes and sizes. A tiny, fragile, sick little angel named Ashley came into our lives and changed us forever. She was born on a beautiful spring day. Our expectations were high that life would be

A Good Time to Grow   113

perfect. But before we knew it, we were on our way to a children's hospital for what became a 19-day vigil.

Ashley taught us many valuable things in her short life: The importance of saying "I love you," of appreciating every moment and of sticking together as a family. We prayed together, hugged each other, laughed and cried.

Ashley showed us how to love and let go and trust in God's mercy. We learned how unimportant material things are. In less than three weeks, Ashley warmed our hearts and changed our lives. When asked how many grandchildren we have, I reply, "We have eight living and one little angel."

Turning Points

*The great thing in this
world is not so much where we are,
but in what direction
we are moving.*

—Oliver Wendell Holmes

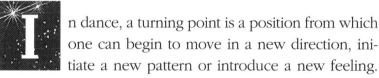n dance, a turning point is a position from which one can begin to move in a new direction, initiate a new pattern or introduce a new feeling. The dancer may leap, spin, glide, step or even be lifted in that new direction, according to what is called for. This new direction, pattern or feeling can transform the dance.

In the dance with destiny, we don't often know what is called for when we reach a turning point; many times we don't even know we have reached a turning point.

Turning points can sometimes come to us through an

116   Transformation: Becoming More of Who We Are

event or person or situation from nowhere to confront us with a situation we didn't ask for or expect. These wake-up calls are actually positive signals and we must be careful to recognize them as such. Too often we miss the signal. Perhaps our lives are too busy or there is too much emotional static. Sometimes we are numbed by medicators such as alcohol, drugs, workaholism, food addictions and gambling.

In this unfeeling mode we can't discern the message of the life force. As a matter of fact, a wake-up call is about the death or end of our will and our control—not about the actual death of a person. Wake-up calls are great opportunities. We can either Band-Aid our own attempts to control or we can abandon control, surrender and begin a vital life of opportunity.

As we learn the lesson of surrender, we give up the idea that there are quick fixes or the possibility of controlling all our events. We come to know that our responsibility will become our guide to an awakening or change of direction.

Life does not give up easily. Something happens to get our attention. If we don't listen to gentle wake-up calls, they become more urgent. Trauma hobbles most people but it wakes others up and energizes them.

By introducing us to turning points, these wake-up calls focus our attention on our spiritual path and alert us that our destiny is being revealed. We may have one, two, or many, but each one will take us to a deeper place of knowing what we are all about.

We are invited into the spiritual evolution by cooperating and embracing our unfolding destiny. We find it easier to make order out of chaos and sense out of nonsense. It becomes easier to recognize coincidences and patterns. As we live this way, the turning points present themselves. The pivot points in the divine journey become clearer.

The people featured in this book have met their "turning points" with courage, acceptance and wisdom. They have transformed themselves and given the world the best they have to offer. Somehow, they know their destiny is important not just to themselves, but all those they touch.

Happy Birthday!
(From Paulette)

In my late 20s I developed allergies to certain foods. Because of the severity of my reactions, it was important that I totally avoid even the most minute amount of certain ingredients. My diet became very limited. Candies, cakes, cookies and desserts were out of the question. It was difficult, but I resigned myself and accepted the restriction as part of my life.

One night, a group of my friends took me out for a birthday dinner. While they were making their dessert orders, I had settled back to have the usual cup of herbal tea. Then I saw the waiter approaching with a cake covered with candles. Everyone sang "Happy Birthday." I looked at my friend as though she had lost her mind.

"You can eat this cake," she said. "I made it just for you."

She had found a recipe that was within my diet range. I

was so touched. I had not had a piece of cake for 12 years. She looked at me and smiled and said, "Everybody deserves to have a birthday cake."

This wonderful lady made me feel completely loved.

Computer Angel
(Amy B.)

Karen was a seasoned computer support specialist when I first started my job. She was a perfectionist and very good at what she did. I was completely hostile while inwardly knowing she was right.

In due time, my boss assigned a project that was way above my head. I fell flat on my face and Karen had to finish the project. It was the most stressful time of my entire career. I was humiliated and hated her for doing it right. I was too ashamed to stay in that department and transferred to another department as a computer liaison. She left the company shortly thereafter.

I thought I would never see her again. Then I entered a special night degree program. The people in my cluster group would spend the entire 22 months together until we finished. I walked into the first day of class and lo and behold there was Karen staring me in the face.

At first I was petrified. The symbol of my insecure beginnings in the computer world was staring me in the face. I gradually began to realize that there was a purpose for this happening. First, I was able to see what I despised in me was what she represented. I was able to heal that. We talked and became friends. She is well-connected and has been a very valuable resource for me as I continue my

Turning Points

career and seek out different paths. I solicit her advice and she has become a mentor for me. I like to think that divine intervention brought us back together again to teach me another life lesson.

PART FOUR

TRANSFORMATIONS OF THE SOUL

here is an old adage that death sits on our left shoulder, with its hand poised above, waiting to touch our head and end our life. From time to time if we turn quickly we can see its shadow and be reminded to live each day as if it is our last.

The Gift of Pain
(Ted Klontz)

Having been born with hemophilia, I've had 50 years of coping with an episodic chronic physical condition. Only within the last decade have I been able to start making my condition work for me instead of being its victim.

The change began with a simple question from my wife-to-be: "What effect do you think that having hemophilia has had on your life?"

My instant response was "none." But no sooner had I uttered the words than I realized how ridiculous they were—no matter how much I'd like to believe they were true. Thus began my journey to and through the other dimensions of my chronic condition.

I started by looking for people who shared my malady. At the time there was a small group of men and their families meeting on a monthly basis in Detroit. At the first gathering I asked if anyone had feelings about having hemophilia and how it had affected their lives. My query was met with sincere denial, not unlike my response to my potential partner.

As I looked around the room, I saw that every man there was physically crippled by joint bleeding, jaundice, chronic liver infections, cranial bleeds or other effects of the disease. Even so, the entire room of people seemed unable to recognize that hemophilia also inflicted emotional and spiritual losses.

When I expressed concerns about how the disease might affect marriage, my concern was met with similar denial. The depth of the negation was poignantly illustrated at one meeting in which a man shared that he and his wife of 25 years had become parents and grandparents and "would do it all over again" despite the difficulties.

His dutiful wife said nothing until I asked how she felt. She quietly replied: "I don't think so. It's been so hard." The room fell silent with the hush only a simple truth can bring.

I began asking questions about the emotional impact of this particular chronic illness. At this time there was not much awareness of, and even less written about, this subject. The unspoken message from leaders in the hemophilia community was "You don't want to get into this."

A classic example of this was the cancellation of a workshop on the topic because not enough people had signed up. This was 1984, when the threat to the hemophilia

Transformations of the Soul

community of a blood product supply tainted with HIV was first being recognized.

Thankfully, there were other disciplines that were openly discussing the impact of chronic illnesses on the emotions and spirit of individuals who have the condition, as well as on their families and the institutions that support them.

The leading discipline was the alcohol and drug treatment field, which was greatly influenced by the work of Virginia Satir and Sharon Wegscheider-Cruse. I found that many of the principles they had developed applied to the hemophiliac community also.

I learned that I carried a lot of shame for having hemophilia. At a deep, unconscious level, I felt as though there was something basically wrong with me. Each bleeding episode tapped into this core chronic shame. I also learned that over the years I had built up resentment toward the medical profession.

While I had developed coping mechanisms that had helped me survive the bleeding episodes, I had unwittingly excluded the potential for greater healing. During long hospital stays, I discovered that aggressive patients are often despised and ignored by medical staff. So I became almost totally passive in my treatment process, giving all of the responsibility for my medical care to the care givers.

I also found the tools used by alcoholism and drug abuse professionals were useful in correcting my distorted thinking, learning the language of feelings and changing my self-defeating behaviors. While medical treatment has saved my life over and over again, the treatment I received for my chronic emotional dysfunction caused by my hemophilia was just as important and much more difficult.

The gifts I have been given as a result of emotional healing are many. I remember the time a friend of mine came

Ted Klontz, codirector of ONSITE Training and Consulting in Tucson, Arizona, is also the coauthor of Family Reconstruction. Ted is a lecturer, educator, father, son, husband and friend who loves the outdoors, bakes wonderful bread and delights people with his sense of humor.

to the hospital, took my hand and held it, said "I love you," stood up, kissed my forehead and left. Because of my openness, I could feel the healing energy of love.

The physical pain of a "bleed" with hemophilia can be excruciating. My awareness of the pain created the opportunity to perform this exercise which provided needed relief. I imagined that all of these pain signals were messages from my body to my brain that "something was wrong."

I pretended that each of the pain signals was a little person whose only job was to keep my body alive by reporting what wasn't right. I spent a lot of time calling them to a meeting in my head and letting them know their message had been heard and acted on in every possible way.

I told them that I needed time to heal and they could take a break. Amazingly enough there was no more pain. When it did return, I would take whatever action was necessary to alleviate it by shifting body positions, adjusting an IV line or getting some rest.

One of the most significant gifts of this emotional healing was being more open with my wife and children about my feelings and theirs, and about my condition and its implications for their lives. I also believe that my emotional healing has improved my physical condition so much that I have not had a "spontaneous" bleed in more than 10 years. Prior to my emotional treatment, they were occurring every autumn, which was the anniversary date of a number of traumatic losses.

I believe that this is a result of reduced stress, which came from greater awareness and expression of feelings, closer monitoring of my physical and mental states and acceptance of my condition and its impact on me and those close to me.

They say that to teach is to learn again. And to share one's experience is to have another chance at experiencing the world anew. Telling the truth about what is going on in our lives is a step to renewed joy.

Out of Pain, Joy
(Ruth Fishel)

I had just completed the first of two workshops called *Stop, Do You Know You're Breathing*, a program I was developing to help high school kids deal with stress, self-esteem and the many problems our young people face today. As the group filed out, one young man approached me nervously. It took a great deal of effort for him to speak. I asked what was bothering him.

"How do you get back to the smooth places," he asked. "My brother committed suicide five months ago and life is ragged and rough and broken up. Can you help me make it smooth again?"

I paused, filled with his pain and mine. I put one hand on his arm.

"I'm standing here, doing what I'm doing, sharing my story," I said quietly. "I'm able to go on with my life. And it's been three and a half years since my son Bob's suicide. I'm proof it does get better. It takes time."

I knew it wasn't the answer he wanted to hear. I suggested he try support groups like Compassionate Friends and A Safe Place. I knew I couldn't help with his pain, but I knew time would. As he walked away, I asked myself how I got here, doing this work.

I was here because I, too, had suffered deeply and had been given the grace to share with these students some of the things I had learned on my own journey to recovery. That reminded me of another time I had asked the same question while returning from teaching a meditation class at a women's prison.

"How did I get from being a nice, Jewish suburban housewife and mother to helping women in prison?"

Of course I knew the answer. I was only one drink away from ending up there myself. Or in a mental institution. Or dead. That recollection led me further back in time, to when I was sitting at my kitchen table at 2:30 in the morning, my only companion a bottle of Scotch. I was writing a

Ruth Fishel, M.Ed., CCAD, LMHC, is the author of several books on recovery; her most recent is Take Time for Yourself. She is also the co-founder of Serenity, Inc., a meditation teacher, national presenter, retreat leader, therapist and co-creator of programs for women at Spirithaven of Cape Cod.

poem, "Good-bye My Friend," to the bottle. I could not give it up. It was, I thought, all that I had left to live for.

"How did I get here?" I asked myself as my writing become more and more indecipherable and my thinking more distorted. I thought that giving up drinking was the end of my life, not the beginning of my journey back from hell.

When I was in my greatest pain, when I could no longer drink or live without drinking, I was finally forced to turn to a power greater than myself for the strength I did not have alone. I was able to stay away from drink for one day on November 27, 1973 by asking for help from a God I did not believe in. Then I began asking for knowledge of God's will and the strength to carry it out, as I now do every day.

It was not long before I was writing and speaking about recovery and helping others on their journeys back from hell. Today, many years later, I understand the sayings "Bloom where you are planted" and "When life gives you a lemon, make lemonade."

When we transform our pain into a gift, we continue to heal. We lighten our own burden while shining a light on the path of healing for others. I have found that by sharing my story with others, I have been able to experience more joy and love.

First, *we need to be honest.* Denial blocks healing.

Second, *we need to ask for help* through prayer and meditation. God speaks through people. We need to surround ourselves with positive, loving and spiritual people and let them help us.

Third, *we need to take whatever time we need to heal.* We must be as gentle and loving and forgiving as we can be with ourselves and let go of any blame, shame or resentments.

And fourth, *we must become willing to help others,* sharing our own strength, hope and experience. Then we will feel a richness and purpose in our lives and a connection to all people in the universe, for, as David Whyte has said, "through the rawness of our wounds we touch the world."

When tragedy touches our lives, others who can help us through heartache and hardship often appear. When we see these people as angels, we tend to want to pass on the gifts of caring, comforting and compassion that we received in our need.

Pass It On
(Nancy Smith)

It is only when I look back on the twists and turns of my spiritual development that I can see some of God's handiwork in the tapestry of my life's journey.

When I was growing up in the 1950s and 1960s, I attended the Episcopal church, which was then steeped in the old English tradition of "Thee and Thou and Thine." Each Sunday service contained a confession that I'll never forget: "We are not so worthy as to gather up the crumbs under Thy table O Lord."

I really felt that unworthy in church, as I did in the rest of my life. My father was autocratic, abusive and very critical of my siblings and me. I saw God in a similar light, as punitive and patriarchal. I felt so unworthy of God's love that I fainted during my confirmation at church. I just didn't feel that I qualified as a fully committed adult church member; I was afraid of being disowned.

When I was 16, my parents divorced and I was finally free of my father's harsh domination. Living with my mother allowed me to enter into a period of rebellion in which I rejected as many rules and regulations as I could, including the doctrines of my religion. For the next 15 years, I spent very little time thinking of God or my faith. I scoffed at religious people and I basked in the many blessings I enjoyed, believing they all came from me.

Not until my early 30s did I begin to encounter losses too great for me to handle on my own. I lost my best friend and my dog within six months. I thought I was going to drown in despair if I didn't seek help.

I visited many churches, but I didn't find one that felt like home until I returned to an Episcopal church, where I found a new updated service and a loving, welcoming God. I felt like the prodigal daughter returning home after a long, wayward absence.

Shortly after, I married and started a family. I attended my husband's church but I didn't know many people there and I wasn't active in the activities it promoted. I felt carefree, thinking God would take care of me now that I was back in his fold. I didn't have to do much except believe in him and go to church.

Then in 1985, my sister's nine-year-old daughter was abducted while walking near her home. There was no trace of her and Sarah is still missing today. The horror of this event was so devastating that my father collapsed like a cardboard box.

When I finally moved past the shock and denial of what happened to my niece, I alternated between grief and rage at God. How could he have let such a horrendous thing happen to this innocent child? Why didn't he protect her?

The authorities told my family that children Sarah's age are usually sexually abused and murdered. When I wasn't dreaming of finding Sarah, I was having nightmares about how she must have died. I couldn't pray; I could only cry or fume at God. I felt so lost and alone; there would be no closure because there were no answers, no body, no funeral, no healing of our wounds.

I didn't ask for help because I didn't think anyone could save me from this trauma. But as God would have it, I got help anyway. The pastor's son, who befriended my son, heard of my ordeal. Someone also told him I left the church in tears every Sunday.

Even though there were more than 1,000 members, the pastor reached out to me. He asked me if I would meet with him each week, and he walked me through my rage

Nancy K. Smith, a licensed clinical social worker, has worked as a therapist, supervisor, consultant and administrator over the past 25 years. As a group leader for Onsite Sierra Tucson, she leads the humor workshop for Time Out for Women. A single parent of a teenaged son, she also volunteers for her church and her community, skates, walks, runs, dances and travels.

and sorrow. He encouraged me to be angry with God and he helped me build an adult faith.

I was so touched by his compassion and his attentiveness that I often think of this man as the shepherd who left his flock to find the lost lamb who had gotten caught on the rocks. I credit him and this experience for planting the seeds of my faith today.

Now, more than a decade later, those seeds have flourished into a strong, deep faith that does not buckle under the weight of tragedy or other misfortune. I believe that God provides his presence, not protection, during painful times, and this presence comes through other people.

I have also come to believe that my faith must be put into action; worshipping and believing isn't enough. If I hadn't been ministered to in my time of need, I wouldn't now be involved in a prison ministry in which I take inner city children to visit their mothers who are serving time in a nearby prison.

These families usually cannot afford to pay for transportation that far away, and not seeing their children is the harshest part of the mother's punishment. When a mother asks me why I take one Saturday a month, without pay or expenses for gas and tolls, I tell her that she matters to me and to God. If that's not enough, I tell her the story of Sarah and finding my faith.

I am also a trained stand-in minister in my church. I sit with people in spiritual crises, walking them through their sorrow and rage. I try to pass on the gift that I was given, when I needed it most, so many years ago.

The Serenity Prayer asks for the serenity to accept the things we cannot change and the courage to change the things we can. Acceptance is a daily effort that also requires enormous courage and rewards us with the peace to savor the brilliance life offers even in the midst of darkness.

Living on the Edge of Acceptance
(Linda Apfelberg)

In many stories of transformation, there are dramatic turning points. Often there is a "magical" event or recognition

Transformations of the Soul

that signals a particular change has occurred or is about to take place. My own evolution has been slow and without fanfare or fireworks.

Many of us live our lives adjusting to the fact that we lie in wait. What an ominous and heavy burden that would be if we awoke each morning and said, "Today is one day less to live, one day closer to death."

We adjust and learn to live within the confines of our own mortality. We learn to live with anxieties, anger, pain and frustrations on a permanent basis. These become a constant presence with a tenacious grip.

I am 55 years old, a wife, a daughter, a mother and a professional woman with graduate degrees who has worked all her adult life. But my story is not a pretty one. I was raised in New York City and spent the last two decades in Manhattan. I was divorced at 22 and remarried when I was 40. As a result of the first, short-lived marriage, I had one son, an adorable, personable but feisty baby whose father chose to deny his existence.

My little boy grew up in an extended family consisting of my mom, my dad and myself. He adored my father. Gramps was a successful trial lawyer, a wizard with words who could light up a room with his presence.

At age four, my son began to exhibit some unusual behavior patterns—he punched, screamed and ran away. I attributed this to the problems of a one-parent family, rejection by his father and being spoiled by doting grandparents. In order to avoid confrontation, grandma and grandpa gave in to his every whim.

He was a bright, highly verbal little boy with a knack for getting the right answers in school and talking his way out of difficult situations. Eventually, his terrible temper prompted me to seek help. I called social agencies, sought psychiatric advice and had endless medical evaluations. We tried all the suggestions to no avail.

Everyday life became problematic. My dad took his grandson to Disney World, to provide some respite for the family. As my son grew larger and stronger, I sent him to special schools and camps, for my benefit as well as his.

The downward spiral worsened with emergency calls to the police for protection from his rages. Broken bones and bruises at his hands were not unusual. Still I looked for help, but found no solution for my son, myself or my parents. I would have given my son away if I could have. It was suggested that I remand him to the courts to protect myself, but I refused, believing that would do irreparable harm.

My father died the summer my son turned 15. He was the last one to see Gramps in the hospital; he had snuck in to see his beloved Gramps. The day of the funeral my son was high on drugs.

Grandma took up Gramps' role as protector with an obsessive drive. Her rewards were physical abuse, blackmail and heartache. The entire family tried an intervention, not with my son but with my mother. Her enabling had made things worse, her life was truly in jeopardy and she was powerless to control it.

The day I remarried, my son punched my new husband in the nose and broke it. My husband, already a steadying presence, intervened in a physical altercation between my son and his grandmother. The blow my husband took was intended for Grandma.

In time, my son became a heroin and cocaine addict and ended up in jail. Each time we would begin to secure some kind of help for the drug problem, my son ran away and would end up in one of three places: jail, a psychiatric ward or intensive care.

Transformations of the Soul 137

Eventually, my husband and I moved to the Southwest. We refused to be taken in by my son's desperate calls for money. Instead, he would appeal to his grandma for money, and she would give it, over and over again. Once a proud lady, she cajoled friends for loans, borrowed on credit cards and took penalties on term deposits.

Now in her late 80s, my mother is nearly destitute. She has not been to a movie, a beauty shop or a social event in nearly 20 years! She will lie and cheat to give my son money the same way that he lies and cheats to get what he wants. His addiction is to drugs, her addiction is to him. They are both addicts.

In the course of his life, this young man has cost his family close to a quarter of a million dollars in bail, psychiatrists, special schools, facilities and legal fees. What it has cost in terms of emotion, spirit, energy and broken relationships—not to mention dreams—cannot be measured in numbers.

Many years ago we realized that help in extricating him from the myriad of lies and deceits was beyond our scope. The one thing that all professionals had said was, "Your son must sink to the very bottom. Only he can ask for help."

My great fear is not that my son or my mother will die, but that their lives will be like living deaths—his ravaged by drug use, hers by heartbreak. I don't have any answers, but I do ask how much does a family sacrifice for the benefit of those who do not want help?

If I am not strong enough to live my life—even with the uncertainty and heartache of the future—my contributions to myself, to my husband and to all that I hold worthwhile, become severely limited, as does the richness of my life.

Linda G. Apfelberg is an educator, consultant, lecturer, writer and adjunct professor in art history at the University of Nevada.

I must admit that I have no control over the generation before and after me, and the relationship they have with each other. By admitting that I have no control over their lives, I have taken some control over mine. There are no easy answers.

I will continue to survive, grow and flourish because in my heart and soul I know I owe that to me. But with the growth there is always faltering and times of tremendous sorrow, hurt and anger.

Transformations of the Soul

We are all the products of our pasts. For some, trauma suffered as a child can destroy the possibility of joy in later life. For others, who accept that they are not alone and that there is someone or something helping them at every step, nothing can stand in the way of a life well lived.

We Are Never Alone
(Robert Ackerman)

He didn't like the way I ate, so I had to eat my meals sitting on newspaper on the floor in a corner of the kitchen. When no one else was home, he would make me stand against the wall in the kitchen. He would sit in a chair on the opposite wall, point a shotgun at me and pull the trigger. Luckily the gun wasn't loaded. When people were around, if he didn't like what I was doing he would get a knife and publicly threaten to castrate me. I was in a foster home. I was five years old.

I was alone. Or was I? I'm in my late 40s now and I remember all these incidents as if they just happened. I have always been in awe that somehow I managed not only to survive, but also to accept my experience without it ruining my life.

I don't know if it is possible to have a transformation at age five, but I do know that what happened would have affected me differently had it not been for one recurring thought as I stared down the barrels of the shotgun. I truly believed that the man was wrong.

Knowing what I know about child abuse professionally and personally, it is usually the child who wonders, "What did I do wrong? Why don't they like me?" It is always a self-indictment that victims place on themselves and it is one of the hardest things to overcome. In my case, I firmly believe

Robert J. Ackerman, Ph.D. is Professor of Sociology and Director of the Mid-Atlantic Training Institute at Indiana University of Pennsylvania. A consultant to the Suzanne Somers Institute and a Fulbright Scholar, Ackerman is also the author of numerous books, including Perfect Daughters *and* Silent Sons.

that I recognized that it wasn't me. It was him. Was I intelligent enough at five to figure that out? I don't know. What I do believe is that someone was looking out for me.

For me, that someone was God.

People have many notions about God and many ideas about religion. Mine have never been very complicated. Quite simply, I believe that I am never alone. This helped me through many problems in my life. It is a quiet feeling that I will endure, that things do make sense and that my Spirit will survive. It has allowed me to be at peace. I consider this the gift of a lifetime.

Today my life is full. I take nothing for granted: I welcome each the day, I appreciate friends, I love being alive and, most important, I adore my family.

Spirituality is not something we get, it is who we are, with all our human strengths and limitations. It's not so much a matter of finding something spiritual outside of us as it is finding what keeps us from recognizing our own spirituality. Sometimes we must find out the hard way that only by keeping the connection between our mind, feelings and body are we able to connect with our spiritual power. It's a connection that undergoes constant change as we deepen the bond between the God within and the God universal.

Moving into the Moment
(Father Leo Booth)

I have always talked about "my moment" as if there were only one. Actually, there have been many turning points in my life. I grew up in England. My mother is Anglican, my father is Catholic and my childhood was filled with their vicious quarrels about religion. Although I didn't know it at the time, the moment when I told my sister "God is tearing our family apart" was probably the most pivotal of my life. It set me on the road to the priesthood, to alcoholism and to my subsequent identification of religious addiction and abuse.

The car crash that caused my Bishop to get me into treatment for alcoholism opened the door to another

Father Leo Booth, CAC, CEDC, is a parish priest in California and the author of When God Becomes A Drug: The God Game. Father Booth is a pioneer in the field of spirituality and recovery from addiction, depression and low self-esteem.

point. Filled with ego, grandiosity and shame, I was packed and heading out the door of my treatment program when a salty old drunk named Harry confronted me. "Leo, you're full of it," he said, "but you can change."

Many people had told me I was full of it. But nobody ever told me with such certainty that I could change. I call those flashes of insights "Harry moments." They happen when someone or a situation puts me squarely in front of myself, shows me who I am, and then reminds me I can change.

Understanding and embracing the ability to modify my behavior has become the foundation of the work I do now—not only with myself, or people in recovery, but with anyone seeking healthy spirituality. I take a Harry moment and say to my church, to my religion, "You're full of it, but you can change." I say it to my staff, my friends, to myself.

There's a lot to the saying that "I'm a work in progress," for I now understand that spiritual growth is an ongoing process, and I will always be changing, evolving, transforming. I don't expect I'll ever be "done."

I suggest a first basic step of identifying the messages that have shaped your beliefs about yourself, about God and how you fit in the scheme of things. I realized that I had a very disconnected relationship with God the Father that was similar to my relationship with my Dad; everything went through Mother Church as it had with Mum. Then I saw how this worked in other parts of my life.

Today I work on keeping the direct connection with my "God within" and the "God universal" open and flowing and give thanks for my Harry moments.

People often look to life's dramatic events for meaning and direction. But it is usually in the everyday struggles to love each other, to make a living, to find our place in the world, that we find wisdom and our purpose in life. It is rarely easy and often painful, but when we pay attention, we find that we all share the same struggle.

Life Is a Do-It-Yourself Project
(Lucia Capacchione)

In looking back at my life, I see not only a trail of twists and turns, but also a pattern: The crises or major changes in my personal life were turning points that always led to transformations that shaped new work in public service. This pattern began early on.

At age eight, I showed extraordinary love and talent for music and began studying piano and composing. It seemed destined: I would follow a career in music. My parents and my piano teacher offered encouragement and support. However, at age nine I got pneumonia and suffered dreadful side effects from penicillin. High fevers and visual/auditory hallucinations left me terrified. Assurances from adults that "these things are not real" were no help. They felt real. While recovering, I received a get-well gift from a neighbor: a how-to-draw book, pencils and a pad of drawing paper. A whole new world of imagination and joy opened up. Drawing my way back to health, I was unwittingly sowing the seeds for an eventual career as an artist and art educator. I continued playing and writing music, but it gradually moved into the background.

The next turning point came with motherhood in my early 20s. Raising two little girls filled me with a passion to know all about how children develop and learn. I observed my own and other children, read and studied and was eventually trained in the Montessori Method of early education. My motivation was more maternal than professional. I wanted to give my children the best possible start in life.

However, in 1965, while serving my classroom internship, I was elected to direct a large program for 300 children in the inner city of Los Angeles—the year of the Watts riots.

Transformations of the Soul   145

The program was the newly created Project Head Start. We were to be pioneers in this new educational experiment. At age 29, I was more surprised than anyone to be honored with the gift of serving on such a grand scale. It started to dawn on me that some power far greater than my intellect or will was guiding my life. The next few years were indescribably active and fruitful as my personal learning meshed with public service to a riot-torn community.

At the end of that period, my life began splitting apart at the seams. My father, deeply addicted to gambling, was hospitalized for manic depression and given electroshock therapy. My mother filed for a separation after 35 years of marriage. At the same time, my husband, with whom I had recently formed a design/consulting company, told me he was leaving me for another woman.

That pushed me to the edge and I considered suicide. If there had been sleeping pills or other drugs in the house that night, I might very well have done it. Perhaps the thought of my children held me back. Certainly, my Higher Self had other plans.

I survived the dissolution of the marriage and business partnership, relocated and carried on with my own career as a designer and early childhood consultant. I entered a 1970s world of dating and relationships so different from the 1950s—the last time I had been single—that I might as well have been on another planet.

Within three years, the string of constant crises caught up with me. I became very ill with a mysterious malady which the doctors were never really able to diagnose or treat. I began reacting to the numerous medications, as I had with the penicillin.

One day the medical clinic called to say that my lab tests had been mixed up with another patient's and I had received the wrong prescription. I was directed to stop taking the medication. I was appalled. And yet this shocking news ushered in the biggest turning point of my life to date. That small inner voice told me to throw away all the medications and find another way. Terrified, I followed this intuitive prompting despite having no idea what the alternatives were.

I was able to listen to my inner self because I had begun keeping a journal, where I poured out all the pain, fear and anger that had been gathering inside. Each day, I continued this inner listening by drawing and writing my dreams, my feelings, my insights into the journal.

I entered the world of white pages which contained all that I could express. The insights and guidance I received through this practice, which I later called the Creative Journal method, led me into therapy, graduate school in psychology and eventually into a private practice as an art therapist. I also taught Creative Journal classes, sharing the techniques I had developed in my own healing process.

Along the way, I pioneered inner child work. Right/left hand dialogues with my own inner child had been a major factor in my own recovery and I used this method with my clients and students in journal classes. The techniques were especially beneficial for child abuse survivors.

Since then, I have written nine books based on Creative Journal techniques for fields such as health, education, childbirth, creativity and inner child work. These books are illustrated by students and clients. Their contributions have given depth and heart to the books. My work as a lecturer, workshop leader and trainer has taken me around the world and allowed me to share tools with people I never dreamed of meeting.

Perhaps most rewarding of all have been the letters and comments from people who have benefited from my work.

Transformations of the Soul

Lucia Capacchione, Ph.D., ATR, is an artist, art therapist, internationally known workshop leader and author of nine books, including The Creative Journal, The Power of Your Other Hand and Recovery of Your Inner Child. A pioneer in the field of healing through art, she is also known for her technique of drawing and inner dialoguing.

"Your story is my story," they tell me. It has been an adventure at every turn, filled with surprises and wonderful, wonderful people. It has been both terrifying and exhilarating, full of self-doubts as well as knowledge that my life and struggles have made a difference in other people's lives.

148   *Transformations of the Soul*

Every person is a miracle, a never-to-be repeated, irreplaceable being with astounding capacity to both endure and transcend pain to fulfill his or her unique potential. Like the caterpillar who becomes the butterfly, we must undergo transformation to become our true selves. But unlike the caterpillar's unconscious metamorphosis, we must choose to let go of the past and test our frail new wings in an unknown and often frightening future.

The Birth of a Butterfly
(Hal Dessel)

Just when the caterpillar thinks its world has come to an end, God turns it into a butterfly.

This image is an archetype of the experience of transformation on the human journey. With the hindsight of recovery, the saying was far more true of me than I could have ever imagined.

"I have to change or I'm going to die." The words choked out of me as I wept with waves of pain from deep inside. I was a 38-year-old Jesuit priest living and ministering on an Indian reservation in South Dakota. I had been ordained for six years and was talking to my spiritual director who had become an older brother/mentor figure in my life. It was late June, 1983 and I was on medication after a two-week suicidal crisis in April. I had left the reservation for a week or two to visit with him and get my act back together.

I was working almost 100 hours a week, ran nine miles a day, even if I hadn't slept the night, drank 25 cups of caffeinated coffee a day while doing home visits and taking part in various meetings. My lunch was six candy bars and a Coke in the car while driving to and from reservation towns. My weight fluctuated wildly from gorging and starving. My tolerance to alcohol was increasing so that 10 beers had no effect. I drank every night just to relax and shut my head off.

I had panic attacks, was physically exhausted, depressed and suicidal. I was terrified of going crazy and exploding in violence. I struggled with obsessions and compulsions about cleanliness and was full of and driven by feelings of shame, fear, anger, relief, hurt and loneliness—all of which I could analyze brilliantly and talk about eloquently and yet still never feel and resolve.

I was leading a double life. I was dying on the inside yet nobody would have known my anguish because I looked and sounded presentable. Even when I shared my pain, I did it so convincingly that spiritual directors, friends, counselors thought I had things pretty well put together. As the gap between what I lived inside and showed outside widened into a chasm, I knew I needed to change or I was going to die.

"Wow, you're really damaged," said the counselor, after a two-hour hot seat confrontation in a group therapy treatment for my alcoholism in September, 1983. When I heard those words, a bolt of sheer terror ran up my spine. He said out loud what I had always feared and felt and fought so hard to suppress.

The world as I had known it ended as I began the long journey of recovery from addiction-dependency. With the help of 12-Step programs, I came to see the root causes of my misery.

I grew up in a painful family system, a repressive, sexually shaming Catholic school and church. As the first-born child, I was placed in an adult world from the start and loved being the center of attention. I learned to play to the audience and developed extrasensory sensitivity to the feelings and body language of my caregivers.

When I stopped drinking and began recovery, I discovered layers of myself that I had never known or felt before: my innermost core, my golden child; my rage-wounded toddler; schoolboy overachiever, both teacher's pet and incorrigible bad boy; terrified teenager and young adult. They were all inside this terrible wreck I had become.

My first two years of recovery were deeply painful. I attended meetings, therapy sessions, workshops and conventions. I saw my spiritual director weekly. I learned time management, assertive communication and relaxation techniques. I read daily affirmations and meditation books and devoured books on recovery.

Even with all kinds of changes, none of them lasted more than six weeks. I still had workaholic binges. I then found therapy in a center that valued me, and taught me about my feeling life. My core healing began. It was like "feeling surgery."

I learned to experience my feelings with all my body, discharge their energy vocally and physically, and to express their meaning with assertiveness and action. Free from my deadly emotional baggage, I realized that I no longer fit in a celibate lifestyle. In 1987, after 23 years with the Jesuits, I became a single man with hopes of marriage. I was 42.

People would ask me if I felt guilty before God for breaking my vows and violating my holy orders. My understanding of the divine will for me had grown very simple; God wanted me to be my true self. All else, including vows and orders, had to be evaluated in this light.

I returned to school and earned a master's in social work. After two years of courtship, I married a longtime friend and experienced a liberating family reconstruction, which

Hal Dessel (pictured with his wife, Judith) is a psychotherapist, dancer, singer, husband, artist. A former Jesuit priest who ministered on the Rosebud Sioux Reservation, he also holds master's degrees in theology and social work.

combines psychodrama and family systems theory to enable people to reexperience and let go of long-suppressed feelings. Today, I enjoy my private practice as a licensed clinical social worker and certified addictions/co-dependency counselor leading therapy groups. I have also been doing Earth celebrations and sacred folk dances with my wife and other men and women in the Milwaukee area. I have also been leading men's retreats.

In short, I am living as a butterfly.

PART FIVE

MESSENGERS, MENTORS AND TEACHERS: MODERN-DAY PROPHETS IN THE EVERYDAY WORLD

When the Student Is Ready, the Teacher Will Appear

When the student is ready, the teacher will appear.

—Buddhist saying

ost dances call for more than one dancer. This is especially true in the dance of destiny and the transformations we experience along the way. No one dances or transforms in a vacuum. We all need accomplices. As these stories of change indicate, inspiration can come from the most unexpected quarters.

All religions have stories about people or events that serve as guides to individuals, as well as entire nations. They go by many names: prophets, messengers, sages, elders and angels. In fact the Greek word for messenger is *angelos*. These are people who walk on Earth and share the truth and wisdom.

Now and then they offer their knowledge and share with many people at the same time. Among the great ones are Buddha, Jesus Christ, Abraham Lincoln, Black Elk, Gandhi, Helen Keller and Martin Luther King Jr. Among those less well-known are Bill Wilson, Virginia Satir, John Smith and Dr. Bob. Many had similar core messages as they addressed the needs of humankind.

Each era produces its own messengers and morals. Some current emissaries are Frederick Buechner, Bernie Siegel, Gail Sheehy, Gloria Steinem, Betty Friedan, Thomas Moore, Richard Bach, Richard Seltzer, Norman Cousins, Steven Spielberg, Marian Wright Edelman and Joan Borysenko.

We also encounter messengers and messages in everyday wisdom and ordinary people. The teachings may be a simple sharing or storytelling—the pages of a book or the example of a life well-lived. There are teachers in 12-Step groups, support groups, Native American sweat lodges, vision quests, spiritual retreats, synagogues, churches, meditation books, sacred circles, the Talmud, the Bible and other sacred writings. They surround us if we care to learn from them.

Tough Love
(Amy B.'s Story)

My teenage years were tumultuous. At age 15, my life crashed when I discovered the wonderfully numbing effect of certain substances. I floated my way through high school. Then, four years later my father died suddenly. We had a strained relationship during my teen years.

Things were gradually getting better, but they were by no means solved. His death hit me like a lead brick. I couldn't handle the pain and guilt for being such a problem and fell back into drug use—the only way for me to cope.

My mother was not only grieving the loss of her partner but also worried sick about me.

Enter my uncle, a physician, who was in town for my father's funeral. He had dealt with substance abuse as the former director of a treatment center. My mother spoke to him and they planned a "mini-intervention."

He asked me to take him to the airport. I'll never forget the conversation we had. Being the youngest and my father's only girl, I had always been coddled and sheltered. My uncle took the direct approach and basically told me I better get my act together, get some help before it was too late. He had arranged for me to enter a treatment program that afternoon.

It was a short conversation, but a life-changing one. It hit me right between the eyes; I understood with complete clarity the road I needed to follow. I remember thinking that my father's life was over, but I could begin mine over. I was being given another chance.

Now at 37, I am a healthy, happy and somewhat well-adjusted individual who owes my new life to my uncle who gave me the turn-around message.

You Never Know
(From Pat)

It was 1981. I was a resident in a halfway house for chemically dependent adults in a large city. This was my first night on a new job in a nursing home and I needed to take a city bus. In the small town where I grew up there were no buses. My peers explained there were two late buses. I had to check the first one to make sure it was the right one. As I stepped from the curb the driver passed right by me, obviously deciding that I didn't want his ride. As I stood on the corner late at night in the dark, big city, I began to cry. Now what would I do?

I crossed the street to a small sandwich shop and called a taxi and explained my situation to the driver.

"I'm an alcoholic, I live in a halfway house, and this is my first night on a new job. I have $2.40, please take me as far as you can and I'll run the rest of the way."

He settled me in the back seat. On the way he drove through a McDonald's and ordered a cup of coffee. From there he drove me right to the door of the nursing home. He jumped out and opened my door. As I reached for my $2.40, he handed me the cup of coffee and tipped his hat.

"Keep your money, lady," he said. That was the best ride I ever had. Not because I didn't have to pay, but because it restored my faith in humanity.

RELIGION
AND SPIRITUALITY

Messengers may or may not be connected with a particular religion. Religion is about humans finding a relationship to God. Spirituality is finding God in other human beings.

I make no attempt to define or describe God. Throughout the ages there have been creeds, theologies, stories, doctrines and dogma that have tried to capture the truths about the divine. Thousands of books have been written and many institutions have attested to the essence of spirituality.

Perhaps the greatest breakthrough is becoming alert to God's presence in the world around us. The Spirit becomes something we can see, hear and feel. And the ways we acknowledge God are as infinite as our own unique destinies. The ways in which we can experience the divine are endless:

The white-capped sea
The smile of a child

The flight of a bird
The love of a parent or grandparent
The wind in the trees
The comfort of a trusted friend
The touch of a lover

You need only look to your own sensations to find how God is revealed to you. What stirs compassion in your heart? What makes you marvel at the intricacies of nature? What gives wing to your imagination?

This letter was sent by a dying woman to her family and friends. It was an inspiring way for her and those she loved to experience closure.

A Letter to Loved Ones
(From Billie)

Dear Loved Ones,

If you are reading this message then you have, in some way, touched my life, and for this, I want to thank you.

These past months have been painful and difficult but, as we've often said "pain is gain." Amid the suffering there has also been much growth. I have experienced an even more intimate relationship with my Higher Power, who has given me strength and courage. I have felt the arms of Jesus around me and have been comforted by the love of his Blessed Mother.

I have had time to reflect on the people and events of my life. I have enjoyed some laughter and shed some tears. No doubt, somewhere along the journey I have thought of you.

Religion and Spirituality 161

Some years back, I learned how to live. Now, surrounded by loving care, I am learning how to die. The hardest thing is saying good-bye, but I am not afraid. I know there is a place for me in heaven with no fear and no pain. As the Bible says, "In my father's house there are many mansions . . ."

I have come to believe that my heavenly mansion has been prepared for me, decorated in my colors.

If I have in any way made any difference in your life, I am grateful. All I really did was say yes to God and allowed him to use me. He did the rest. Each one of you has a special place in life. Do whatever it takes to find that place and your life will be beautiful, no matter what.

Please remember me in your prayers until we meet again. I know we will. Until then, may you have faith behind you, hope before you and love beside you.

Author's note: For many years Billie was a counselor for emotionally battered women and children. She will be remembered by countless people as an angel.

UNIQUE DESTINIES, UNIQUE GUIDES

Individuals in flux frequently encounter mentors who help make the journey easier. Guidance is very important for a traveler on the road to spirituality. Each person has a unique path to self-realization and a single connection with some spiritual power. Each of us is uniquely guided along the way.

But much can be learned from the journeys of others. Pitfalls can be avoided, barriers can be circumvented and mistakes can be detoured. When an encouraging guide maps out the way, the path becomes clearer and the destination seems more certain and attainable. With the map drawn from the guide's own life and journey, with the wisdom of our mentor's experience shared in trust, we can more readily discern the options open to us. We can make informed choices suited for our needs.

Many options are possible for our growth. We live in times where transformation and knowledge are growing in all fields. We need to make ourselves aware of the

164 *Messengers, Mentors and Teachers*

new information in religion, physics and medicine. We need to listen to scientists, mystics, psychologists, executives, physicians, philosophers and others who have contributed to the information explosion.

Messengers are here to connect us together in meaningful ways. We are not meant to live in isolation. They let us know when it is safe to trust; they help us learn our individual destinies. They invite us to feel new feelings and think new thoughts; they bring wisdom.

What is considered creative in each of us is simply a messenger acting within us. Throughout history great poets, writers, scientists and athletes have been people who found the internal message and discovered the gifts that are uniquely theirs. Finding this gift and accepting it has brought many people to greatness they never believed possible.

Messengers didn't start out that way. They, too, had fears and doubts. Their faith grew through experience and by listening to and responding to others that came before them. Finally they got the message! In doing so they found peace, beauty and a sense of meaning.

People have always sought a purpose for, understanding of and meaning to their weary lives. In every culture, every religion and every nation there is a hunger to connect and belong. At the core of our humanity there is a need for togetherness. Basically no matter what our religious beliefs or skin color, we are all very much alike in spirit. As Helen Keller put it: "We are all more alike than we are different."

Messengers can be any age, from any background, tall, short, black, green and white. Sometimes an emissary is recognized only by the miracles left behind. There also seems to be a kinship, a thread, that binds us regardless of situations or distances.

Divine intervention can often be best understood as we learn to recognize the heralds in our lives. They have been around throughout the ages. Chances are we've met several but may not have noticed because we were not ready or did not need the message at the time. As the Buddhists say, "When the student is ready, the teacher will appear." In time, we will all learn to accept that almost everyone in our paths becomes a potential teacher or mentor.

It is important to wait for the basic questions of life to arrive before we look for messengers; otherwise, we have answers but no pressing questions. With the world facing so many pressing questions today, we are in great need of messengers, which may be why there seems to be an abundance of them. Since each one of us experiences the world differently, we need many different types to make sure the news gets through no matter what language we speak or what belief system we have.

An Act of Kindness
(Mary Jo's Encounter)

One day I was stuck in my car in a long line at a toll gate. It was late; I was tired and grew increasingly impatient as I crept up toward the toll booth behind a new blue Buick. When I finally reached the booth to hand the attendant my toll, he grinned and said: "The man who just passed through paid for you, too!"

Suddenly, thanks to the good gesture of a stranger, I didn't feel quite as crabby as I continued my trip home. That unknown, unseen man changed my day around.

Angels Hang Stars of Hope
(John F.'s Story)

I met John H. in 1981 when he was in his early 60s. He had been treated for chronic alcoholism a few years before that. The pain he had suffered had etched in him a quiet spirituality.

We met for lunch. I was doing some work at the local hospital with detoxing alcoholics and wanted to enlist the help of local AA'ers. Before lunch was finished, John H. had quizzed me about my training, familiarity with the field of chemical dependency and co-dependency, my family of origin and whether I had read *Another Chance*.

He quickly produced a copy of the book and suggested that I read it and we would meet again for lunch. Thus began a relationship in which ever so often John H. would suggest that I would benefit immensely from attending a Family Reconstruction.

He offered many opportunities for my spouse and I to learn about treatment for alcoholism, co-dependency and addictive disorders. He arranged funding for us to attend conferences, visit treatment centers and meet leaders in the field. When he would suggest that I would benefit from participating in a Family Reconstruction workshop, I usually responded by saying that after many hours of psychoanalytic

Unique Destinies, Unique Guides 167

therapy I didn't need more therapy. I never told him the truth, though I'm sure he knew. I was terrified of experiential therapy.

The disease process in me blossomed in 1988 in workaholism, co-dependency and alcoholism. When my isolation, grandiosity and emotional numbness led me to suicidal despair, I called a counselor John H. recommended.

"I need to come to treatment," I said.

She replied: "I've been expecting you."

When I returned after a month's treatment, John H. welcomed me back and once again suggested that I attend a Family Reconstruction workshop. He would send both my wife and me. In December 1989, I experienced the miracle of being born again.

John H. walked with me all these years, placing in my life opportunities, people and choices. When the time came that the pain of the disease had pushed me to the door of death, an angel hung stars of hope to reach for.

Author's note: John F. passed away shortly after sharing this story about his own angel, John H. Like his benefactor, John F. leaves behind a great number of people who benefited greatly from his wisdom. He, too, will be remembered as an angel.

My Own Angels

I have known and benefited from many different messengers in my life. And I am very grateful for how their messages transformed my life. These are just a few of my messenger angels. I believe each of us has a flock of angels who have touched our lives deeply.

Martin Luther King Jr.
Inspired me to develop my own dreams.
My grandmother
Told me to remember I was no better than anyone else, but I was always just as good. She cemented my self-worth.
Elvis Presley
Awakened my internal sense of rhythm.
Jesus Christ
Showed me how to love and find courage.

My mother
Let me experience unconditional love.
My sister Sue
Taught me how to create a home.
Virginia Satir, teacher and therapist
Taught me to value people because of their differences.
My daughter Sandy
Showed me how to use time to build relationships.
My daughter Deb
Taught me about commitment and courage.
My son Patrick
Taught me about family values.
Anthony Padavano, theologian
Gently pushed me into several transforming experiences through his writings.
Ted Klontz, colleague and friend
Showed me how to live with chronic illness.
Mary Jo Arnold and Beth D'Atri, colleagues and friends
Showed me how to grieve and laugh at the same time.
Shirley, lifelong friend
Taught me how close bonds can grow over the years, even as people make big changes in their lives.
Gary, teacher
Stretched me professionally in ways I never dreamed possible.
Joseph, husband
Taught me humor, faithfulness, how to create comfort and how to play.
Larry, business manager
Showed me how to handle my financial affairs.

Mentors and Teachers

Modern-day angels are mentors and teachers, helpmates and role models. Like a seasoned dancer who shows a novice new steps, mentors instruct, give information, share their stories and experiences and provide emotional support.

By contrast, teachers are challengers. They may confront us, put roadblocks in our way, challenge us and often make life difficult. They are like choreographers who create a demanding yet dazzling routine. As we struggle to master the steps, we find unrealized strengths. Rising to the challenge is a growing and validating experience. Each encounter with a teacher will change us in the direction of our growth.

Second Chances
(Pete's Tale)

When I was a freshman in college, I believed that everything I did had to be perfect. There was no room for failure and no mercy when I failed.

Luckily, my first semester courses were all pass/fail and the semester was uneventful. The second semester I took a course in political philosophy from Dr. Phillip Haring. I got an "F" on my first paper. I was devastated!

In my typical style, I had worked extremely hard on this paper, putting in long hours, rewriting it many times, agonizing over every word.

I approached Dr. Haring in total trepidation. How was I going to explain this to my parents? How could I stay in school? The thought that I couldn't survive this failure even flashed across my mind.

He patiently explained where I'd gone wrong and listened to my attempts to justify what I had done. He redirected me on every point and taught me what had to be different. My reasoning had been shallow and incomplete; my hopelessness was still profound.

Then Dr. Haring surprised me by letting me know that this paper would not count in the final semester grade. I hadn't asked for this. I hadn't even considered that this could be an option. But it was offered, along with assurances that he saw value in the work I had done.

I'd had my first lesson in mercy. There could be second chances in life.

Mentors

To recognize a mentor, look for these signs:

1. They come in all shapes, sizes and colors.
2. They work behind the scenes to help another and soothe the soul.
3. They come like a light in times of darkness.
4. They become known through acts of kindness.
5. They help make miracles on Earth.
6. They point out our possibilities.
7. They make us feel welcome in the world.
8. They give us direction.

Teachers

Teachers don't always stand in front of a class lecturing. They also . . .

1. Challenge us and invite us to grow.
2. Confront our errant behavior.
3. Make life difficult for us at times.
4. Set up barriers to our plans.
5. Pull out our resiliency and need for strength.
6. Force us to be courageous.
7. Fill us with doubt and force us to clarify.
8. Stimulate parts of ourselves we didn't know we ever had.

BECOMING A MESSENGER

ave you heard these expressions?

"I found that book so inspiring."
"Thanks, you're an angel."
"Keep me in your prayers."
"That message really touched me."

These words have a familiar ring because miracles are available every day. The messengers who bring them are part of our daily lives. In fact carrying messages can become contagious. The more messages we receive, the more we want to become a messenger. The stories shared in this book are about this phenomenon of passing it on—about angelic messages.

We live in a world of brokenness and alienation. This is both a comfort and a necessity for finding connection, peace, beauty and strengths in our daily lives with each other. This is what messengers help us do.

The stories in this book are from grandmas, teachers, friends, mentors—all students of life who have become angels and friends. Their tales make us feel better knowing we are not alone. Their words of encouragement, hope and comfort are gifts.

The ticket to personal fulfillment is within. Sharing can be a divine experience, for the teller and the listener.

In the coming years we will need more people with the courage to speak of their ordeals. As we approach the next century, it's interesting to look back and see the patterns and stages we have gone through.

The 1950s were clearly a time of change. Television shrank the world; we all became each others' neighbors. Curiosity was aroused. The 1960s were a time of internal revolution and external chaos. War, political unrest, civil disorders, family conflicts all reached levels never before seen. In the 1970s we regrouped with the help of the hippies. The self-help movement of the 1980s prepared us for the spiritual movement of the 1990s.

During each of these eras there have been people who made us aware of alternatives and new possibilities: beat poets and rebels without a cause in the 1950s; political radicals and hippies in the 1960s; communes and encounter groups in the 1970s; recovery leaders and self-help authors in the 1980s. With a spiritual renaissance in full bloom in the 1990s, it is no wonder that we look for angels in our midst.

We need to stay in balance as we complete a major emotional transformation. We are often dissatisfied with the spiritual status quo and uncertain where to find the authentic experience. The balance of this decade pulses with the hope that following the way of the Spirit will bring the revolutionary change we need to heal the planet, politically, socially, economically and environmentally. Each of has a role; the universe is asking us all to become messengers. We discover our message as:

It gets easier to know big deals from little deals.
Everything seems clearer.
Living is more satisfying.
New experiences unfold before you.
Challenges appear and you survive.
Coincidences happen.

You become aware of an inner restlessness that feels like excitement.

You must discover the inner message and bring it forth to share. As you explore, embrace and define your destiny, you will have an understanding of your special unique message.

The Mystery of Angels
(Maria's Tale)

On All Saints Day, the darkness comes quickly. I am reminded of the first time I experienced this day in Sweden. I drove around the countryside looking at the cemeteries aglow with candles lighting each and every grave. Such a beautiful and peaceful sight. There was a magical, caring oneness, and a sense of generational belonging. I didn't even think of angels being involved back then.

Almost a decade later, I am surrounded by angels. A cherub sits on the fireplace mantle, two calendars have angel pictures, a cheerful description of an angel sits on the bookcase. I buy greeting cards with angel messages.

Today I believe that angels have been with me all along, even though they are still a mystery. They have been with me in times of despair and aloneness, at times when pain or humiliation seemed unbearable. I am certain that I have avoided troubles by taking a sharp U-turn. Was I warned by angels?

Was an angel present when I left the hospital after spending all day and night there with my dying mother? When I got home the hospital called and said she died just after I left. She didn't want to have me there when she died.

Was an angel present when I was crushed by the weight of a 25-year marriage that ended in divorce? I would gladly have stopped living. How did I go on?

Soon after my daughter told me that she was pregnant. She asked if she should abort. I saw the shining light of the child coming through her eyes and filling the room with a glow. My mother's presence was there. My daughter was smiling. Were angels there, too?

Is an angel watching over my brother who has HIV, and keeping him well? Will they guard him when the time to leave the Earth grows near?

Was my atheist father sent an angel when his angioplasty failed and he had emergency by-pass surgery at age 80? Today he has a caring community of friends, neighbors and family to help him stay independent. His will to survive is strong and his mental powers are clear.

My other brother had a seizure; the MRI showed a malignant brain tumor. He is 48 years old. He went through radiation and chemotherapy and is back on the job as a mail carrier. Were angels with him?

The last of my brothers had a total transformation of his life five years ago after a long addiction. Did the angels keep him alive through those dangerous times?

Did angels sit beside me in rooms throughout the United States, Sweden, Finland, Norway and Denmark when I guided group therapy sessions? The healing powers came, sometimes without my even knowing the language. It wasn't me. It seemed like collective love. The power was so strong. Did it come from angels?

Where is my angel? You are always a bit too far in front of me and too foggy. I want my angel to be beautiful and bright—to give me direction about my mission and help with my new love.

Angels and love are mystery. Every friend that calls does so at the right time. Every hand and hug is placed perfectly. Even the tears of hurt that roll down the cheeks and transform into relief—and into a deeper love and understanding—are perfect.

A Musical Angel
(From Sharon)

As I was wrapping up a one-hour presentation before an audience of several hundred, I set up a multi-media finale. My show called for slides, music and dialogue. The music was to be "Amazing Grace."

The room darkened, the slides began and I was just about to start speaking when the tape recorder jammed and the music wouldn't play. I was panic-stricken.

A few seconds passed. In the dark I felt a presence on the stage; a few moments later I heard "Amazing Grace" being played on a synthesizer. I went into the finale saved by an angel who came to my rescue and averted what could have been a disaster. The angel was entertainer Jerry Florence.

We met after the program and became close friends. For several years after, Jerry traveled with my husband and I professionally. We learned the value of adding music to our training events.

When Jerry died a few years ago, the world lost a special musician and gained a musical angel.

Each one of us will live out our unique destiny. The choice is ours: Accept that we are here to learn to dance with the Spirit; or to stand still when the rhythm of life continually invites us to join in. As author Sam Keen said, this dance with destiny is "the only dance there is."

As we take each step along the way, we may feel a part of our destiny coming to pass. Yet the restlessness of our souls and hunger for the truth let us know there is always much more.

Have faith. Love each other deeply. Love that is honest and giving will make up for failures and mistakes that we all make learning to dance with destiny.

PART SIX

TRANSFORMATIONS OF THE SPIRIT

eople say they want to have a better relationship with God, their Higher Power—whatever or whomever they perceive to lie at the heart of spiritual awareness. Sometimes it eludes them. Others have found absolute honesty is a prerequisite for contact with God.

Honesty Isn't the Best Policy —It's the Only One
(Ann Hardy)

I am now in my 60s. As I look back, I realize that the important transformations in my life have been preceded by a time of loss, pain or deep turbulence. I also see that I've always had a vague sense of the coming "turning point." The tough time always ends with surrender—giving up something I believed necessary in my life.

I have been on a spiritual quest since I can remember. All my life I have pursued a working, enlightened contact with the God of the universe. While I know that God is always present and accessible, it is during times of deep emotional pain or grief that I realize a transformation has taken place. This is followed by an increased awareness and understanding of who I am, who God is, and how spiritual principles operate in my life and the lives of those I interact with.

Certain times stand out more clearly than others. Losing Wendy, my husband's daughter and my step-daughter, was one of them. She was only 14 when she was diagnosed with stomach cancer. Her father, Sam, and I felt it would be better if she came to live with us.

I practiced the gift of love, gained through a former transformation, and soon Wendy and I developed a deep bond. We had wonderful times together shopping and traveling.

When Wendy's cancer went into partial remission, I knew that the love and safety I had given had helped and I decided that she could live if I loved her with all my heart and prayed hard.

One morning I was at breakfast when she came into the dining room. I knew it was growing again and when Wendy died three months later, I held her as she smiled that "wise old lady" smile and said good-bye to me. She sighed deeply and floated away on Wednesday night.

I did not weep or mourn her passing from our lives, for I did not know how to grieve then. Besides, I had been told how strong I was, how courageously I was handling it and I couldn't let anyone know the pain I felt, the deep loss, the shock that my love wasn't enough to heal her. I resumed work as usual saying my prayers and meditations, believing it was God's will, that she was out of pain and in a better place.

Transformations of the Spirit

Ann Hardy is a private therapist in Hawaii, co-founder of Turn-Off Treatment Center and co-founder of House of Hope for Women.

My spiritual life was dry, without feeling. I'd had those times before and passed through them. People were kind to me which almost made up for my barren spirituality.

At Christmas that year, I was watching *Little Women* on television. When the death scene came up, I felt my throat tightening. I went outside to the field behind my house thinking I was going to throw up.

Instead I began to scream. It was cold and windy in that field but I howled, "My God, why did you give her to me, if you were just going to take her away?"

The wind stopped and I was surrounded by light; I knew that I was being spoken to and this is what I heard: "I didn't expect you to like it. It didn't happen to you, it happened to her. She was a gift to you for your learning. She belongs to me and she was loaned to you for awhile."

The light faded away slowly and I went inside and slept, aware that a transformation had taken place. In the following days and weeks, as I pondered the event and this new "contact" with God and the universe, it came to me that I had told the truth!

Some may say, "You can't lie to God." But that's exactly what I did. I hadn't expressed my rage, my pain to the God I understood. I had been a good child, saying all the right things, expressing from my intellect. But the truth in my gut was real. That is what I finally shouted in the field.

Since that time I tell the truth to God: the pain, the anger, the joy, the gratitude, swearing and cussing if it feels right. Along the way I've had bad times, but never a dry, empty time with no spiritual contact. Whatever is happening in my life, my God is there. I know it and I feel it and I'm never alone.

Life is inexplicable and unpredictable. We were never meant to make our way alone, yet paradoxically, we often find it difficult to ask for help.

It's Not Your Fault
(Jerry Moe)

One evening in particular illustrates the shame of my early life. I was 10 and my family dined out at a posh San

Francisco restaurant to celebrate my parents' 23rd wedding anniversary. As everyone ate, I heard the adults' muffled whispers. My dad was getting drunk. I hadn't really noticed because I had been awestruck by the beautiful tables, the band and the dance floor. One look at Dad and I knew they were right.

Halfway through dinner I noticed Dad was gone, but everyone else seemed oblivious. I went to look for him and found him propped against the wall in the rest room. I quickly wet a paper towel and handed it to him. My mind was racing; I was terrified we would get in trouble because Dad was drunk in this fancy place. I took my father by the hand and led him out of the bathroom and steered toward our table. But Dad tugged me in a different direction saying, "A couple more minutes."

We walked down a long corridor and Dad stopped at a set of French doors which led into a large banquet room filled with tables, beautiful white linen and "reserved" signs. He closed the doors and garbled, "We'll only stay here a minute."

As I turned to gaze at the room, Dad proceeded to throw up all over the place. I was so petrified I couldn't move; I was sure we'd get caught and put in jail. I grabbed Dad's hand and quickly headed back to our table. I ate the rest of my dinner in silence and in record time. Whenever a waiter or busboy approached, my heart raced in fear that they were coming to get us. It would be years before I ever told anyone what really happened that evening.

As a child I was filled with fear, confusion and sadness. A primary coping mechanism was isolating myself from those around me, physically and emotionally. I shut myself off truly believing no one was there for me. I survived by staying out of the way and putting on a facade.

But I wasn't a kid anymore. I was trying to take care of my parents, especially my dad, and getting torn-up inside by a constant parade of negative messages, many of them self-inflicted. I was consumed with guilt and shame.

A major turning point was attending my first Alateen meeting. Oh, how I resisted going, even though my life was falling apart. I had convinced myself there really wasn't a place where I belonged. One look at the lady running the meeting confirmed it. An older woman, she seemed out of step in this group of teens. I thought she didn't have a clue.

Once the meeting began I was overwhelmed by her presence. I couldn't take my eyes off her and soaked up every word. Gladys' eyes appeared to acknowledge my pain and confusion. Her occasional nods, her gentle touch, the warmth of her smile and her soft yet persistent encouragement allowed me to open up in a way I had never done before. I startled myself by telling her things I promised to never tell anyone and letting her and the group hear my pain and see my tears.

She responded by telling me it wasn't my fault. While I had heard those words before, that day they penetrated deep into my soul and I experienced a heavy weight lifting off my shoulders. I sensed a newfound energy. In less than 15 minutes I came to completely trust this woman. I had found a place where I belonged.

Gladys helped me open doors that I'd locked; she guided me to a path I still journey today. She walked me through that difficult first step and stressed my lack of power over the family disease. Gladys showed me how to let go and I soon became free to love and care for myself in a way that allowed the very playful part of me, the child part, to re-emerge. Slowly, I began to heal. One of the toughest early challenges was letting go of my father's

Transformations of the Spirit

disease while continuing to love him even as he went on his last, fatal binge.

Even though our paths only crossed for a short time, Gladys changed my life forever. Today I'm unaware of any greater tribute to give to this angel and to my Higher Power who brought her into my life.

For many years I've experienced joy and gratitude in carrying out this work as an educator, children's therapist and prevention specialist. My life has been blessed with Michelle, a creative and loving wife I adore, and three children who teach me many lessons. Their warmth and acceptance is a far cry from growing up in fear and uncertainty.

The changes that flowed from Gladys' presence in my life also prepared me for dealing with the fear and pain of melanoma. I was able to find the courage and strength to accept God's will for me and I had the wisdom to know I couldn't do it alone.

This ability to reach out deepened my relationship in ways I had never imagined. Michelle held me as I cried. I had always demonstrated my love to her, but too many times I had become caught up in the day-to-day grind and had taken her for granted. I cried with my daughters and held them as they expressed their sadness and fear. I told them how proud I was to be their dad and we eventually laughed about the many happy memories we'd shared.

My son remained stoic until we were alone in the car. He asked me if I was going to die and I honestly replied, "I don't know." He was finally able to cry and share his real feelings with me. Every friend and family member to whom I reached out was loving and supportive. I was making peace.

Today, I have a clean bill of health as the ramifications of this wake-up call continue to unfold. I have a greater clarity

Jerry Moe, Director of the Children's Program, Sierra Tucson, Tucson, Arizona, is the author of Kid's Power: Healing Games for Children of Alcoholics and Discovery: Find the Buried Treasure: He is a lecturer, trainer, son, husband, father and friend.

about my choices and priorities. I'm taking even better care of myself. I want to spend time with my family and surround myself with healthy, positively oriented people.

I appreciate that each day is precious and cherish my closeness with my Higher Power. Most importantly, I realize these gifts from my brush with cancer aren't tools for dying, but for living one day at a time.

There is an old saying that to live is to change; and to have lived well is to have changed often. Dealing with a chronic illness brings changes that aggravate the struggle we all face in balancing dependence and interdependence. We all want to be our own person, to be loved and needed and meet the needs of others.

Claiming My Power
(Virgilia Moran)

After rearing five children, I was looking forward to having some time for myself, a less hectic life with few responsibilities. Shortly after my 53rd birthday I was diagnosed with myasthenia gravis. The diagnosis was a jolt to my consciousness, a wake-up call to my soul.

We were on a long-awaited family vacation. Our whole family was planning to sail across the English Channel to France, through the French canals to Paris and to the Mediterranean. It promised to be wonderful, 88 days with my family on a 39-foot sailboat with no television or telephones.

The first cloud on my horizon came during the cold, windy Channel crossing. I can still remember looking in the mirror one morning and seeing my left eyelid down. I couldn't raise it. I blamed it on the wind and cold.

When the symptom didn't go away, I began to worry and called the doctors at home for advice. I decided to cut short the trip and return home for medical attention.

It was confirmed that I had myasthenia gravis, a chronic neuromuscular disease that involves the weakening of the voluntary muscles. I soon found it difficult to chew and talk. My facial muscles, arms and legs became affected.

Treatment included radical surgery to remove the thymus gland and medication to bring the disease in remission.

Learning to live with a chronic illness is not easy. I had to work through denial and minimizing my condition and accept that I had an illness that will not go away. My body's strength and vitality, taken for granted for so many years, had changed overnight. I was forced to listen to what my body was telling me.

The difficulties started even before the actual onset of the symptoms. I was convinced there was something going on in my body but I was unable to communicate this effectively to several doctors. I felt discounted and gave up trying to explain what I was sensing.

Looking back, I learned how important it is to believe in your own personal experience and to not doubt your own reality. In the future, I will insist on being listened to and search for a doctor who will look beyond the words I use.

Another dilemma I experienced at the beginning was not making my health a priority. Why didn't I return home immediately to receive the medical help I needed? I struggled with many conflicting feelings at that time, refusing to accept what was happening.

How could I not be part of this great family adventure? I felt they needed me. In fact, they could have survived nicely without me. In retrospect, I abandoned myself and was a poor role model for my children.

At first I tried not only to deny the disease's existence but to fight it. I found myself giving into my weakness and letting negativity control me. A turning point for me was when my neurologist said to me that he thought I was afraid of my illness. He tried to convince me that I was in charge, not the illness. It took me a few years to really understand this.

Letting go and forgiveness are two fundamental truths I

Transformations of the Spirit

had to embrace in order to heal. If we let go of things, our life has to change. I think that sometimes we fear death more than we fear change. Change was essential to deal with this illness and the limitations it imposed. Listening to one's body rhythms is crucial.

I know I did not take care of my health in the past. As a mother of five children I was constantly busy. When exhaustion set in I did not listen. I chose to keep going, even though my family didn't really demand it. Chronic illness forced me to choose. Do I remain a victim and never heal, or do I see my illness as a messenger and listen to it?

An illness can be a gift in disguise. Myasthenia gravis forced me to take time out, to reflect and listen to my body. I began to be in charge of my own health. I realized that to commit to wellness I had to strengthen my spirit, stop mourning the death of my past self and concentrate on where I was to go from here.

I realized one does not have to go backward for strength—I already have within me all that made me strong. If it worked in the past, it will work again. I began to be comfortable with my own pace. No longer did I feel I had to keep up with the pace of others.

Chronic illness also forced me to evaluate my personal goals. I took time out to establish and accomplish goals for myself that I had put off: To read, study and listen to good music. I went back to playing the piano, which I loved as a child.

I began to take notice of nature and the beauty around me that I took for granted. I saw my family and friends in a new light and began to cultivate meaningful friendships. I concentrated on the quality rather than quantity of time I spent with loved ones. I am grateful for their love, support and understanding.

My chronic illness also affected them; in a way it became

Virgilia M. Moran lives in Paradise Valley, Arizona with her spouse, Bob, and five children. Besides being a wife, mother and friend, Virgilia is a registered nurse with a bachelor of science in health arts and a master's degree in counseling from Northern Arizona

theirs. Many feelings surfaced—anger and disappointment when I was unable to keep up or participate at all.

At times I thought it was necessary to seek counseling and help my family deal with my limitations by education through literature and videos on myasthenia gravis. This made what I experienced on a day-to-day basis real for them.

A friend once said treatment and healing are like getting on a boat to cross a river but the danger lies in not wanting to get off the boat. One can get stuck, always wanting to be in treatment and process. To really heal and commit our spirit and body to getting well, one has to get off the boat when it reaches the other side.

Trying to improve your life simply by correcting current difficulties is like putting "a Band-Aid on a boil." Healing involves getting to the root of the problem, cutting losses and getting on with life. Most importantly, a spiritual belief system gives the inner strength needed to make the process work.

Becoming Whole Again
(Kathryn Findley)

By the time I finally asked for help I was a 38-year-old wreck. I needed to be free of my alcoholic/abusive husband's behavior. I had absolutely no idea how I had gotten myself into such a pickle, especially since I had spent most of my life trying to please others.

On the outside, we looked like a very successful family. We were well-educated and well-off. Our children were either in college or private schools. We had a lovely home, a condo on the beach and a cabin in the high Sierras. We enjoyed using our own airplane, motorcycles and sports cars and traveled wherever we wanted. But under all of the glitter were two very sick people.

On the inside I was lonely—filled with guilt and shame, terrified, whipped, battered and broken. Unlike many people with Multiple Personality Disorder (MPD), my story is not one of unspeakable horror. Rather, it cuts to the core issue of MPD, which is fear of abandonment.

It was present from before my birth; my parents had considered aborting me. Then I was "hidden" for six months after I emerged. As a child I awoke from naps to find myself totally alone. I was rejected by my siblings so completely that my only playmate in the family was the dog. I once came home to an empty home when my family moved and forgot to take me with them. I also survived incest.

It was the life of a modern-day Cinderella. I was responsible for all of the chores while my siblings did whatever they wanted. One Saturday, I threw a fit about having to clean the house alone and barely survived my sister's attempt to strangle me while our mother was out shopping. Needless to say, I did not request assistance again.

I barely graduated from high school because by then my MPD was fairly well-developed, though still undiagnosed. One personality would attend class, another would do the homework and a third would take the exam. The same personality didn't always perform the same task. The overwhelming loneliness and sense of failure prompted three serious suicide attempts by age 17. No one in my family even noticed. I simply woke up very late in the afternoon feeling sick, alone and behind on my chores.

After my last attempt, two things happened: I developed a closer connection with God and the alter-personality named Kathy emerged. I felt more connected/bonded to "something" and a little safer. Kathy took control and maintained that control over me and the other alters almost all the time for the next two decades.

Nursing school was a respite from the rejection by my family, but it provided a hotbed of activity after-hours for my MPD. Because I only switched alters after-hours, I was able to graduate from nursing in the top 10 percent of my class.

I joined the U.S. Navy Nurse Corps during the Vietnam war. There I met and married my Prince Charming. But instead of living happily ever after, I became a battered wife.

As it turned out, my husband's alcoholism was a blessing in disguise. By the end of 1982, I was in Al-Anon and he was in AA. I was encouraged to go with my husband to an outpatient alcoholism program. It was through these programs that my journey for recovery began and my wholeness was restored. Later, I attended workshops that helped me solidify my work in the recovery process, to reclaim my inner power and to teach me how to use my God-given gifts and talents to my best advantage. In other words, to make good choices.

I experienced two major turning points in treatment: One was realizing that my body and my mind experienced everything and I didn't need to spend time trying to figure out which personality did what. The other was simplifying my life.

Another major turning point was a workshop on Alcoholism and the Family. The speaker's explanation of a dysfunctional versus a nurturing family gave me hope for the future. When I stood to give her a standing ovation, my husband pulled me back down into my seat.

"Don't you ever pull me down again!" I told him.

Later, my husband said, "Do what you need to do and get better so we can live the way we did." He was asking the impossible.

During the next five years I walked away from our marriage and affluent lifestyle and I married a gentle man who gave me one wonderful year during which I learned about love between a man and a woman. He then gave me a year of agony as he tried to recover from his gambling addiction. Our divorce in 1986 was extremely painful.

Even though I tried to protect my assets from his disease, I had to repay all of his debts or go to prison. One of my daughters and I lived on $100 a month for more than a year while Mafia goons threatened us.

Kathryn Findley is the author of Whole in One. *As a result of her personal journey and search for a true healthy life (physically, emotionally, intellectually, and spiritually), she has proven herself to be an accomplished and empathetic teacher in the fields of recovery from addictions, co-dependency and other dysfunctional family systems. Kathryn and her husband reside in Edwards, Missouri, where she founded Sweetwater Retreat. Professional Weekend Workshops were developed to assist the emotionally wounded in recovery and to present them with the tools to build a stronger personal foundation.*

Throughout my recovery, my family disowned me—including my own children. The fear of abandonment that drove me to MPD as a child had become a reality. With the emotional support from my friends and family of choice, I continued to grow and began to experience self-love, self-worth and much improved choicemaking abilities. Surprisingly, I married again!

Now I have peace, serenity, love, victory and freedom to be me. I'm doing the work I enjoy; my husband and I have set up our farm as a productive pig and cattle operation. I have published a book on how to recover from MPD and I am now giving workshops, consultations and lectures. Several professionals and friends have joined with me to expand Sweetwater Retreat to encompass all areas in the art of health and balance.

I am developing new friendships with all members of my family of origin. In fact, each of my children has thanked me for staying true to my resolve, which is setting an example for them to follow on their own journeys of recovery.

There are still challenges; some are intriguing and fun, some are racked with pain. But that's life! In the end, I am grateful to God for the people he brought into my life. They provided the instructions I needed to be able to experience all life has to offer me as a balanced whole person. My hope and prayer is that the insight gained through my recovery may be instrumental in the diagnosis and recovery for others suffering with MPD.

From the Book of Ecclesiastes by way of a 1960s folk song we get these words of wisdom: "To everything there is a season, a time to plant and a time to reap, a time to give and a time to receive."

The Beaver's Wand
(Frances Yerger)

For 17 years I had given my heart and soul to helping young people find themselves and meet life's challenges with self-esteem and self-assurance. Along the way I completed a Ph.D. program, designed a peer counseling network and established very successful summer youth workshops.

At the end of one summer a few years ago, my husband and I took our staff of more than 40 to our home in the White Mountains of Arizona to celebrate their volunteer service to their peers in the summer programs. It was also the end of a season of my life. I had been diagnosed with lymphatic cancer and would soon begin a daunting personal journey.

Even though surrounded and supported by loving family and friends, I felt quite alone, settling into a solitude that told me I must do this healing alone, from my spirit deep within. As we closed the summer with a final celebration, the peer leaders talked about the harmony and integrity I had helped bring about in their lives, saying it was now my turn to receive. My work, they said, was like beavers building homes in harmony with nature.

The group then presented me with a beautiful six-foot-tall aspen stick, carved as a wand, from a sacred beavers' pond in the Apache mountains near our home.

"You will always be our friend and we will support you every step of the way," said one of the leaders. "The Beaver's Wand carries the love and friendship of us all."

It was truly a miraculous moment for me. Tears flowed and the aloneness I had felt began to lift. I knew I needed to let people love me.

My Beaver's Wand has been with me every step of the way through three and half years of grueling treatment—

Transformations of the Spirit

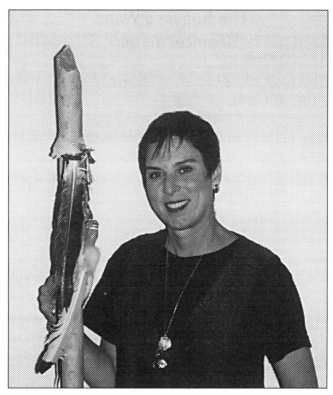

Frances Yerger, Ph.D., is a therapist, mother, leader and humorist. Her work has helped hundreds of young people move into adulthood with confidence and leadership skills. She and her husband Fred enjoy fishing, cooking and entertaining.

with interferon, 10 rounds of chemotherapy, a bone-marrow harvest, 25 weeks of radiation and several surgeries. In the process, the wand became my friend, a real presence in my life.

"She" helped me talk about my disease and constantly reminded me of the love and support of friends who held, blessed, prayed with and endowed this stick with their sweet energy. She has been with me on 22 round-trip flights from Scottsdale to Houston, in hospitals and laboratories and in doctors' offices. People have made room for her, respected and welcomed her. When I told my doctor the story of the wand, he wanted to place his hand on it and empower the wand with his willingness to help me heal.

In fact, she has never been turned down, and this for me is a symbol of people's friendship, caring and love. My Beaver's Wand has not only helped me make new friends, but also to learn and teach new lessons. I love her and what she represents about the love people can and do share.

There is an old saying that "God doesn't give anyone a cross he can't carry." There is much truth in these words. But the saying would be complete by adding these words: "with the love of his family and friends and a lot of prayer time to help carry it."

Motherhood: A Never-Ending Turning Point
(Delores Eischen)

I graduated from high school in a small town in southwestern Minnesota. My plans to become a kindergarten teacher never became a reality. Instead, I became a young mom and raised nine children—one son and eight daughters, four of whom became teachers.

I was married in January, 1949 at age 19 and moved to a farm where my first daughter, Peg, was born. Ten months later, Barb was born. At first I was unaware that Peg had Down's syndrome. She needed extra care and medical

Transformations of the Spirit

attention; she was three before she walked and five before she was toilet-trained and able to feed herself. At eight, she went to a state school. That was a very difficult decision and proved to be a turning point in my life.

Our only son, Kurt, came 18 months after Barb. Our fourth child, Linda, was born 17 months later. With four in diapers and three on bottles there was little time for relaxation. We had no indoor plumbing or running water, so we carried it and heated it for washing clothes, dishes and baths. I also prepared meals for my family and—at spring planting, haying and harvest—as many as five extra hired hands. There was lunch, dinner, afternoon lunch and sometimes supper. Thank heavens you could prop up baby bottles, especially during meal times. There was also housework and laundry to do—with no washer or dryer.

We never missed church on Sunday, even though my husband and I went at different times. I didn't drive, so my in-laws would pick me up for church then take me back home to prepare Sunday dinner which was always something special.

In December, 1955, I had my first miscarriage and had a great deal of hemorrhaging. After surviving this trauma, I realized my prayers were being heard and God must have plans for me to continue as a mother and provider. Over the next 10 years, I had five more daughters. Each was a turning point and an opportunity to affirm my faith. There were many times I needed it.

Our daughter Linda had a ruptured appendix two weeks before the arrival of our last child, Roxane. We almost lost Linda because of the rupture, but with the care of doctors, aunts and friends and many hours of prayer, we knew God was among us again. At age 13, our daughter Joan was diagnosed with juvenile diabetes. More turning points.

In 1965, my husband, then 41, suffered a severe heart

attack. With a farm with 100 head of cattle and numerous chores to manage, plus eight children under the age of 16, prayer became more important than ever.

The doctors said my husband couldn't manage heavy physical labor so we managed a liquor store. During those five years, I gave birth to my ninth child, a little girl. Eventually, my husband went back to farming.

With nine children I became involved in many school activities and church gatherings. I also became a member of the church choir once again and helped start a religious program for our high school students. As my children grew, I started day care in my home plus local baking for people for a little extra income. In 1975, I took a job as a cook in a small, rural parochial school. I was very fortunate to start each morning by attending Mass, which became very important to me.

Three years later my husband had a serious farm accident causing a blood clot to the brain which required surgery. Again, God was at my side. Two years later, I had an irregular heart rhythm and was sent to the hospital to have the heart stopped and put back into pattern. I was also informed of the possibility the heart might not start. Once again my life was in God's care. Turn, turn, turn.

There are 32 members of our family. We are very close. On one memorable gathering my husband remarked he didn't feel well and stepped outside for a breath of fresh air. He wound up dying that day of an aneurysm. I must admit I was very angry with God at this time. It took several months to realize it was through prayers and God's care I was able to go on with my life. As my youngest daughter Amy was away at college, loneliness was a challenge and still is.

I returned to my job at school and the following year

Transformations of the Spirit

Delores Eischen is a lay leader in church, choir member, mother of nine, widow, sister, aunt and grandmother. She and her family have made countless contributions in the lifestyles each has chosen.

once again entered the hospital with fluid on the heart and a damaged mitral valve. I underwent open heart surgery. Not three days later, I was operated on again for a staph infection.

Today I am a lay presider in my church and also belong to the choir, bake for others and do child care. I'm very proud of my life and our accomplishments throughout the years. Many years were difficult, sacrifices were made but we were able to put eight children through high school, vocational-technical school and college.

I feel I'm blessed to have the love of my family and friends who are always near when I need them and thank God for letting me enjoy the sunrises, sunsets, rainbows and even dreary days. I put my life in God's hands each morning.

Many of us lose touch with that inner knowledge that we have a still, calm center, no matter how overwhelming our circumstances. Sometimes the healing power of humor can be discovered after decades of emptiness.

I Am Responsible for How I Feel
(Yvonne Kaye)

I was just short of six years old when the turmoil of World War II began. As I swam in a sea of silence, I made two important decisions: I would never let anyone love me and I would die.

What flowed from those two critical survival decisions constitutes the major turning points in my life. Today I am loved as I never thought imaginable and have a lust for life I did not think possible.

The transformations that unfolded began in the late 1960s, those far-off halcyon days, when skirts were full and bras were burned. My husband at the time had already left England to live in the States and I followed with our four small children. After six miserable months in the Philadelphia area, with homesickness a constant companion, a woman visited me and asked me to read a book. She felt it would help me, but since I was unable to concentrate I thought it highly unlikely. Over the next several weeks she persisted, and finally I agreed to read it just to shut her up.

I am sure it sounds banal, but the book changed my life. There were many turning points before, after and still continuing, but this was the big one! The book, *Man's Search for Meaning*, by Dr. Viktor Frankl, astounded me. It still does. Written in a concentration camp, Frankl observed that people make conscious decisions on the way they feel. I did not know that. The six-year-old child was still in control of me and my attitudes. Her fears were paramount in abandonment and rejection. Yet here was a brilliant man in such dire circumstances who could write these words: "They can do anything to my body but they cannot touch my thoughts."

I could not imagine such courage, but then I did not accept my own. I read the book over and over again. It is not easy reading. The brutality always attacks the soul, but the message is simple: I am responsible for how I feel.

It took about six or seven years to reach my subconscious where the work is done. In the long term it has meant that I have become the architect of my own internal home. This notion has freed the magnificent spirituality given to me at birth and which now sustains me in the delight of living.

Today I speak on spirituality and humor, integral parts of my working and personal life. I finally accepted that people make conscious decisions on the way they feel.

A major turning point was my delicious humor which I both cherish and embrace. Although many of my original attitudinal changes came from suffering, I now look to the

Yvonne Kaye, Ph.D., has been in the field of human service since 1951. She has been in private practice as an addictions consultant, thanatologist and specialist in relationship problems since 1970. Since 1990, on the publication of her book Credit, Cash and Codependency: The Money Connection, Dr. Kaye has become nationally known as specializing in the area of financial/codependency treatment and prevention. Her book 366 Encouragements for Prosperity establishes her as a national motivator. Her mission is to alleviate stress and increase mental, physical, spiritual and emotional wellbeing: to train others to continue and expand her methods of discovery.

light. I know why I became a bereavement specialist and why I am good at it. However, I also know I do not have to experience every form of suffering in order to relate. Thanks to The Compassionate Friends, I have learned exquisite humility and receive deep love from them which is entirely reciprocal.

My children have taught me the power of humor in all its glory. We have major challenges in our family, tuberous sclerosis, multiple sclerosis and when we are sad about these issues, there is always Viktor Frankl. He does not believe that one should minimize one's challenges, but face them and go on. And so we do, with laughter as a primary ingredient.

Accepting love from many people is a way of having turning points every day. The love of my life partner reminds me daily that laughter is a gift from God. I say "A-women" to that!

Life is one long conversation with oneself and with others. Sometimes the noise made by all the voices inside our heads makes it impossible to hear what others are saying. But when we are ready to hear the words come from outside, not the committee inside.

Stop Wiggling
(Joe Cruse)

Be still, and know that I am God.

—Ps. 46:10

I drank alcohol for 25 years. For the past 23, I have been sober. God willing, I will soon have lived more years sober than drinking and drunk.

I have always felt my troubles acutely: as a little kid I cheated at games or threw temper tantrums; as a teenager I found it hard to cope when my girlfriend rejected me and when I lost the election for class office. As I grew, so did my problems and the intensity with which I felt them.

I would have gotten drunk as a youngster if I had known how. I still remember the shame of what I did when I spotted my dad at the only junior league ball game he ever attended. I tried to steal second base with two outs and the ball in the pitcher's hand and ended our season with one rash move to get attention.

I suffered in misery until I was 18 and met my true love—alcohol. I fell head over heels; it was the solution to my problems and numbed the pain of living.

Inside I was a mess—filled with fear, anxiety and a powerful need to be noticed. I felt small and weak and unsure and desperately wanted to be big, strong and right without anyone finding out how insignificant, unsure and afraid I felt. I kept my secret belief that I was chosen by God to be someone very special under lock and key.

My father was, by most standards, a success. Everyone in our small town seemed to love him. I deduced that being loved was what led to wealth, which led, in turn, to excitement, attention and even power. I wanted them all.

They said I was my father's son, right down to my love for drink. I looked like him, I walked like him and I made sure that I acted like him. My skewed fairy-tale view of life was based on direct observation of just one family—ours. I pretended, and later came to believe, that I had great power and would gain love and respect from my parents and the world, if they would only notice me.

So I acted in plays, did volunteer work, debated and substituted for the local minister twice when he went on

Transformations of the Spirit

vacation. I even became a doctor because being in the medical profession was a huge attention-getter.

Despite my efforts, I never felt noticed enough. So I learned to wait. I spent many hours sitting at the foot of my dad's chair while he read the paper and drank his alcohol, waiting to be noticed.

I waited for hair to grow on my chest, for physical strength and courage, for signs of my future. Throughout this time I had a deep yearning, but it had no "why" or "what for."

Alcohol became my special emotional medicator. Nicotine was its assistant, providing good maintenance and support. As I grew older, I began medicating at an increasing rate with both frenetic activity and alcohol. As my fears increased so did my habits: more alcohol, more work, more accomplishments, more spending, more control over family and others.

My drinking went from moderate to extremely heavy as I moved from college to medical school and then on to the service. I left the military after nine years with a flask in one hand and grandiose plans for a Family Live-in Cancer Hospital in the other. I decided to build a specialized medical center in California and wandered up and down Wilshire Boulevard in Los Angeles to raise money. Frustrated by day and drunk at night, I finally settled for setting up a private practice.

Weekends and out-of-town trips were filled with drinking episodes. Three years before I began my actual recovery, I was taken to Alcoholics Anonymous, but I continued to run my own program. I called myself a "sipping slipper." I tried Antabuse combined with a teaspoon of bourbon. The 20 minutes of Antabuse reaction—severe flushing, rapid heartbeat and panting—was better than sitting alone and yearning. I would call myself out of self-help groups with my beeper, take my Antabuse cocktail and drive around alone, dodging disaster and waiting. The loneliness grew deeper.

The month I spent at a nationally recognized treatment center had its impact on me, but not immediately. I began using pills and became my own physician and pharmacist. I now realize that when alcohol and drug abuse landed me in the hospital, my own attending physicians didn't know what to do with me, so how in the world could I?

I have practiced medicine and surgery for 35 years. As a physician I have made many case presentations to my colleagues. As a recovering alcoholic physician I have naturally been interested in presenting teaching cases that pertain to the disease of alcoholism and drug dependency.

My experience shows that physicians neither know how nor want to diagnose alcoholism, especially in a colleague. Alcoholics are admitted to hospitals but the underlying cause is not mentioned. This silence can be due to ignorance, a well-intentioned desire to cover-up, a personal distaste for people suffering from alcoholism, and the fear of legal recriminations, embarrassment and/or confrontation.

Attending physicians are often unknowing, unwitting and unwilling. Here are a few examples of how doctors have attempted to care for an alcoholic colleague:

A 27-year-old physician was admitted with a diagnosis of therapeutic misadventure due to rabies vaccine injections, manifested in arthritis, fever and an allergic reaction at the injection sites. He had also been on a three-day drinking spree.

A 31-year-old physician was admitted following an auto accident. He had a concussion, acute strain of the cervical spine, multiple contusions and lacerations of the face and right knee. A colleague removed a blood alcohol slip from his chart. The judge reduced the charge to careless driving.

A physician, age 38, passed out at a Christmas Eve party and was rushed by ambulance to the hospital. The attending physician was a friend who knew that the patient was drunk. He sent him home the next morning and wrote on his chart: vaso-vagal syncope (fainting), myositis (chest pain), and flu syndrome.

Perhaps the most serious case was a 40-year-old emergency room physician. Alcohol was obviously involved in the patient's suicide attempt. He had jabbed a steak knife into his chest just below the heart. The injuries were repaired and a week later he was discharged without any staff attempts at discussion or intervention. The final diagnoses were just the bare facts: knife wound, left chest; exploratory laparatomy and thoractomy.

These cases are important because I was the patient in every one of them. There were no interventions for my alcoholism, just good intentions. My doctors were unknowing, unwitting and unwilling, and so was I.

My days of dodging disaster almost came to an end as I lay on that operating table with a self-inflicted knife wound. These friends of mine were preparing to put me to sleep, open my chest and abdomen and save my life. I squirmed with shame because I couldn't even commit suicide.

In her haste, my favorite scrub nurse dropped a large metal retractor onto the marble floor. It prompted me to jump and pull again at the wrist straps and declare through clenched teeth, "Damn it, I screwed it up again. I can't do anything right."

Joseph Cruse, M.D., was the founding medical director of the Betty Ford Clinic and the former medical director of Onsite Training and Consulting in Tucson, Arizona. He now enjoys traveling, singing, dancing, computers and having fun with his soulmate, Sharon Wegscheider-Cruse.

She shot right back: "Shut up, Dr. Cruse, just lie still and stop wiggling!"

All my life people had been telling me to hold still and stop wiggling. I finally accepted that it was time to listen and begin the long-delayed, joyful process of healing.

Transformations of the Spirit   215

Sometimes all that is required of us in the dance of destiny is that we keep moving forward, even when it seems all is lost.

Just Keep Walking
(John Jarrard)

In 1977, I moved to Nashville, Tennessee, to pursue my dream of becoming a country songwriter. I took a job as a motel desk clerk to support my family and didn't have much time to write songs.

In May 1979, complications from diabetes began to create difficulties with my vision. A year later the doctors said they could do no more. I was totally blind. I went through months of soul-searching before deciding to pursue my dream.

With the help of a mobility instructor, I learned to get around using a cane and the bus system. For two years I rode almost daily to the offices of music publishers to play songs I had written. I heard "no" more than "yes." Finally, in late 1982 I was offered my first staff writing job; a year later my first hot record followed, "Nobody But You," sung by Don Williams. Over the next few years, four more hit records followed.

And so did further complications from diabetes. This time my kidneys were affected.

The complications threatened my overall health, which in turn jeopardized my songwriting, my marriage, finances and emotional stability. I was as low as I had ever been, feeling lost and uncertain. It took until spring 1989 for another turning point to change my life again.

One morning instead of writing I went for a walk. For reasons I still cannot explain, I asked my wife to drop me on Music Row, a request I had never made, and began hoofing it back home. Within a couple blocks, I accidentally placed my cane under a bench and snapped it in two.

I was miles from home and felt helpless. I have long since given up trying to explain what happened next. I heard a voice clearly direct me to just keep walking. The words repeated themselves the instant I questioned them. So I obeyed. It was difficult to trust the process, but after a few blocks it felt almost natural.

As I approached the major intersection, I hesitated, and was again reassured, "Just keep walking, son, you're doing fine." After making it across six lanes of traffic, I relaxed and felt so confident I refused a ride from a friend. She later reported that I looked so comfortable she had not even noticed I didn't have my cane.

I was serene knowing that everything would be fine. I wish I could tell you that everything worked out, but nothing is that simple.

The marriage could not be salvaged; a difficult divorce and financial distress ensued. My career bottomed out. My health continued to suffer, culminating in kidney failure and more than a year of dialysis treatments. Throughout it all, I was able to return to that walk and that voice of assurance.

I walked a long way before the situation turned around, but when it did, it did so in a mighty way. A kidney and pancreas transplant eliminated the need for dialysis and insulin injections. My career rebounded with six more number one records; I married the woman of my dreams and we are busy building the kind of life of which I always dreamed.

Transformations of the Spirit

John Jarrard lives in Nashville, Tennessee, where he thankfully makes a good living writing songs. Besides writing songs, he counts his wife Janet, his daughter Amanda, his stepson Matthew, a number of dear friends and kin, Winston Cup stock car racing, old guitars and home cooking high on the list of things he loves.

I have had and will have problems, of course, but I am secure in the knowledge that I have been, and always will be, guided.

In the face of tragedy, humor can help heal the soul.

Bottom of the Pit/
Top of the Mountain
(Beth D'Atri)

Transformation has woven itself in and out of my soul as I have journeyed through a myriad of life events. Sometimes I have been given choices and sometimes events are thrust upon me, cutting me to the core. Change has come in bits and pieces that are both lightning bolts and divine intervention.

Having been born into a family with a history of addiction, I struggled for years to control my life and the lives of others. Domination worked in some ways but was generally ineffective in bringing me the perfect life. Letting go instead of trying to control has been a hard lesson but worth the rewards of greater peace of mind. And I have finally learned that my role is to do the footwork and leave the outcome to the Higher Power.

Letting go of fear has been a critical area of change for me. At 46 years of age, with my marriage near divorce, I knew I had to address the core issues of my life. My counselor told me that fear seemed to be my Higher Power. I was miffed that this woman would presume such a thing and dismissed her remark as wrong.

I was in the process of attempting to develop a relationship with Higher Power through my co-dependency recovery program and I was sure that fear was certainly NOT my Higher Power. Yet since childhood my life has been built on fear—fear of not being liked, fear of not being perfect, fear of abandonment, fear of not being good enough.

Facing my dread was a huge challenge and one that I had avoided at all costs. It was much easier to point my finger at others and say if only he or she had acted differently my problems would be solved. Moving from fear to trust has been an incredibly painful journey because I had to allow myself to become vulnerable and let others support and guide me. I have had to learn to trust that life leads us in certain directions which are not always clear and are part of a much greater plan.

In 1995 I faced the greatest challenge of my life when my husband of nearly 30 years underwent two brain surgeries and open heart surgery. Later that year my 22-year-old son committed suicide. I had to dig deeper than I ever thought possible. I was brought to my knees, faced with letting fear back in, choosing anger over courage. All that I had learned on my journey was needed to get through my monumental grief. My sorrow was too deep to put into words.

A wise woman named Edna once invited me to open my heart. My inner wisdom and intuition told me I must trust her to get through the debilitating pain. To open my heart I had to let Higher Power in at a much deeper level. By paying attention to the different forms—people, events, books, inspirations and what seemed like coincidences—I was able to survive.

My husband has a new lease on life and I'm grateful for his courage and persistence in facing his enormous struggles. In the death of my son I have been challenged to choose bitterness or acceptance. How could I ever come to accept suicide? How could the Higher Power have given me such a heavy burden when I have tried so hard to be a good person?

Beth D'Atri is a counselor at Park High School in Livingson, Montana and a part-time psychotherapist at Onsite in Tuscon, Arizona. She has a B.S. degree from Texas Tech and a master's in counseling from University of Michigan. She conducts retreats, hikes, camps out in the hills of Montana.

Sometimes I wish I had never written the special prayer that I say each day as I drive to work near the majestic mountains of Montana. It goes, "Higher Power, I give you my life and my will. I ask that you give me strength and courage, wisdom and knowledge so that I may do your will for me."

The suicide of my son was not what I was asking strength and courage for. I meant typical daily life events, not something so devastating. My path has made me look death squarely in the face, and cope with it the best way I can.

Transformations of the Spirit

With each day comes new light, new understanding, new trust in the process of life. As time passes, I have come to a deeper acceptance, a letting go, a trusting that Higher Power knows better than I.

I cherish more deeply my relationship with my loving family, my many dedicated friends and myself, whom I have grown to love more and more with each passing day.

Closure

Those who believe are tempted to only believe what fits with their preconceived ideas and values.

Those who have faith, however, open their minds to truth, happenings, turning points and surprises.

Truth involves both pain and pleasure and the seeker who chooses to experience both will know the fullness of life and will be introduced to the dance with the Spirit.

Listen for your personal music and enjoy "the dance."

Bibliography

Ardell, Donald B. *High Level Wellness.* Emmaus, Penn.: Rodale Press, 1977.

Cerutti, Edwina. *Olga Worrall.* New York: Harper & Row, 1975.

Chopra, Deepak. *Unconditional Life.* New York: Bantam Books, 1991.

Friedan, Betty. *The Fountain of Age.* New York: Simon & Schuster, 1993.

Martz, Sandra Haldeman. *I Am Becoming the Woman I've Wanted.* Watsonville, Calif.: Papier-Mache Press, 1994.

Jaffee, Dennis T. *Healing from Within.* New York: Simon & Schuster, 1980.

Link, Mark. *In the Stillness Is the Dancing.* Niles, Ill.: Argus Communications, 1972.

Other Books by
Sharon Wegscheider-Cruse

From Science and Behavior
Palo Alto, California
(1-800-547-9001)

Another Chance: Hope and Health for the Alcoholic Family,
1981, 1989 (also in German)

Experiential Therapy, 1990

Family Reconstruction, 1995

Grandparenting, 1996

From Health Communications, Inc.
Deerfield Beach, Florida
(1-800-851-9100)

Choicemaking, 1985

Learning to Love Yourself, 1987 (also in French)

Coupleship, 1988

Understanding Co-dependency, 1990

Life After Divorce, 1994

From ONSITE
Tucson, Arizona
(1-800-341-7432)

The Family Trap, 1976

Understanding Me, 1995

The New Classics

#424X — $12.95

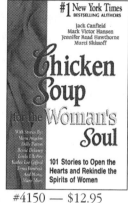

#4150 — $12.95

#4630 — $12.95

#262X — $12.95

#3316 — $12.95

#3790 — $12.95

Selected books are available in hardcover, large print, audiocassette and compact disc.

#4142 — $8.95   #4215 — $8.95

Available in bookstores everywhere or call 1-800-441-5569 for Visa or MasterCard orders.
Prices do not include shipping and handling. Your response code is **BKS**.

INSIGHTS FOR *Personal Fulfillment*

Celebrating Success

In this unique four-color book, 150 well-known men and women define what success means to them. Each entry—originally written on personal letterhead—is as unique and inspiring as the person who wrote it. This thought-provoking collection will give you new insights and ideas about how you can define success in your own life. Contributions come from John Glenn, René Russo, Troy Aikman, Robert Schuller, Jack Lemmon, Chris Evert and many, many others.

Code 455X, paperback...............$12.95
Code 4703, hardcover $24.00

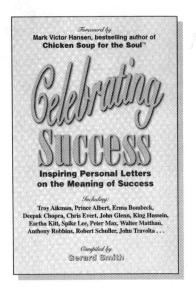

ABC's for Living

Sometimes the best things come in small packages, and *ABC's for Living* is no exception. This thoughtful gift book is a compilation, from A to Z, of beautiful and wise essays for crafting a life that is abundant and meaningful. *A llow yourself to reach for the unattainable.... Believe in something greater than yourself.... Choose to make a difference....*

Code 4584 ....$8.95

Health Communications, Inc.®
The Life Issues Publisher

Available in bookstores everywhere or call 1-800-441-5569 for Visa or MasterCard orders.
Prices do not include shipping and handling. Your response code is **BKS**.